THE STORY OF
ANCIENT CHINA

SUZANNE STRAUSS ART
The Fay School, Southborough, Massachusetts

PEMBLEWICK PRESS
Lincoln, Massachusetts

TO STUART
With warm gratitude for our deep and lasting friendship

Once again, I must express my thanks to Dick Upjohn, Teacher Emeritus of the History Department of Fay School, for carefully reading and commenting upon my manuscript. I am continually amazed by the depth of his knowledge of ancient history, and I am extremely grateful for his insights and "gentle suggestions," which have been so helpful in making this book as accurate a record of ancient China as possible. And once again, I am deeply indebted to my husband, Bob, Professor of Politics at Brandeis University, for patiently and painstakingly going over the final draft of the manuscript.

Other Books by the Same Author
EARLY TIMES: THE STORY OF ANCIENT EGYPT
EARLY TIMES: THE STORY OF ANCIENT GREECE
EARLY TIMES: THE STORY OF ANCIENT ROME
EARLY TIMES: THE STORY OF THE MIDDLE AGES
WEST MEETS EAST: THE TRAVELS OF ALEXANDER THE GREAT
QUINTET: FIVE LIVELY PLAYS FOR KIDS
THE STORY OF THE RENAISSANCE
ANCIENT TIMES: THE STORY OF THE FIRST AMERICANS (BOOK I)
NATIVE AMERICA ON THE EVE OF CONQUEST: THE STORY OF THE FIRST AMERICANS
  (BOOK II)

TABLE OF CONTENTS

TO THE TEACHER

As the 21st century begins to unfold, China stands at the center stage of world politics. This vast nation promises to be a critical player in the events that will affect our planet for decades to come. This in itself is a prime reason for American children to become familiar with the economic and cultural traditions of modern China. But an even greater reason is the tremendous richness of Chinese civilization.

This book is intended to introduce middle school students to China's evolution from earliest times through the "Golden Age" of the Tang dynasty. (The Tang dynasty is considered the transitional period between ancient and modern China.) As the title of the book suggests, emphasis is placed upon the story element of history. Your students will witness an ever-unfolding drama of events, where ambitious leaders seek forceful ways to put their ideals into practice, while others look for more peaceful means to enrich their own lives and those of the people around them. It's an exciting story, filled with a wide range of characters — kings, emperors, generals, concubines, eunuchs, artists, inventers, poets, laborers, craftsmen, and hard-working peasants.

With the exception of Chapter 4 (THE GREAT PHILOSOPHERS), each chapter focuses upon a specific time period. All chapters conclude with review questions and activities designed to enrich a student's understanding of the materials he has read. References are also made to important contemporary happenings on the world scene. I strongly suggest that you allot plenty of time for each chapter. In my classes, we often read a section of a chapter aloud together, questioning and debating major points as we move along. Sometimes we spend an entire period on a single page. For example, a passage on poetry is an opportunity for a general discussion of the differences between Chinese and western forms of verse. References to dragons and unicorns open a window for a "mini unit" on the mythical creatures of the ancient world. A controversial figure invites role-playing, a fun way to bring history to life. And as you conclude each chapter, be certain to carefully review the highlights of that particular time period. The history of ancient China is an extremely complex one, but a slow and careful study of it will open untold vistas for your students.

Of course, it is important to have a good collection of resources in your classroom — history texts as well as richly illustrated books about art, poetry, mythology, literature, architecture, world geography, and anything else that will enhance a student's grasp of Chinese history. Do make use of the many websites available on the Internet as well as the wide selection of Chinese music now available on CD's. Most of all, have fun with your students as you venture through the rich tapestry of events, discoveries, and achievements of ancient China.

INTRODUCTION
THE MIDDLE KINGDOM

In our modern, high-tech world, everything seems to be in a state of constant change. Computers quickly become out of date as newer, faster, and more powerful models replace them. In these fast-paced times, anything that hasn't changed for awhile — like the friendly neighborhood general store, for example —is often viewed as quaint and old-fashioned.

This book is about a place where the basic patterns of life, the beliefs, and the customs remained pretty much the same for over 2,000 years! China holds the record for having the longest continuous civilization in the world. Although other ancient cultures began earlier in Egypt, Crete, and Mesopotamia, they eventually fell apart or were destroyed by outside forces. Chinese civilization withstood every invasion and continued to thrive, undiminished! Even today, many traditions of ancient China are still going strong.

The Chinese have always loved keeping records, and they have provided historians with highly detailed accounts of all major events since very early times. In this book, you will see that much of their history is divided into dynasties (periods when China was ruled by generations of a single family). The first emperor came to the throne in 221 BC. For virtually the entire period of recorded European history — up until 1911 — a grand total of 157 different emperors ruled China.

The ancient Chinese called their land *Zhongguo* (pronounced Jong Gwo), which means "Middle Kingdom." They were convinced that they lived in the center of the world and that all other people — the outsiders — were barbarians. Occasionally, "foreigners" did settle in the Middle Kingdom and learn Chinese ways. They, too, became civilized. An ancient proverb expresses it well: "China is a sea which salts all rivers that run into it."

The ancient Chinese did have a lot to be proud of. They were an amazingly resourceful people. Not only did they create a very efficient form of government that would endure for countless generations, but they also invented all kinds of useful tools and products — like paper, the com-

Chinese maps traditionally had five directions — north, south, east, west, and center.

pass, gunpowder, printing, silk cloth, wheelbarrows, umbrellas, and kites, to name just a few. And they were remarkably creative. Poets and painters created works of art that rank among the greatest world treasures, while Chinese scholars created philosophies that still shape the lives of vast numbers of people.

At the dawn of the 21st century, China's population is over 1.2 billion. That's nearly one in every four people on the planet. More people speak Chinese than any other language in the world. But the fact that China is major world power is only one reason to learn about it's history. As you'll see, the story of ancient China is a fascinating tale, filled with colorful characters — fierce warlords, gentle monks, haughty emperors, clever empresses, poets, artists, musicians, philosophers, soldiers, peasants, and silkweavers, to say nothing of the dragons, unicorns, and other mythical creatures. Interested? Then let's begin!

How to pronounce Chinese words

The Chinese language has no alphabet. The spoken language depends upon the use of tones, such as a rise in the voice or a fall. The way a syllable is pronounced affects its meaning. There have always been many dialects of spoken Chinese, the system of tones varying from one to another. Since 1949 Mandarin has been the official dialect of the government, schools, and the media.

Despite the variety of dialects in the spoken language, the written script is standard and can be easily understood by people from any region of China. In fact, China has the world's oldest system of writing that is still in use. It is made up of over 70,000 characters (symbols). An average person has to master from 3,000 to 4,000 characters to read a newspaper.

Pronouncing Chinese words has always been a challenge for English speakers. In the 19th century, the Wade Giles system was invented to put the basic sounds of spoken Chinese into the letters of the Roman (Latin) alphabet. But this was a very complicated system. In 1956 the Chinese government introduced a new way of writing standard Chinese phonetically in a Latin script. It is known as "Spelling Sounds," or *Hanyu Pinyin*. It's generally known as "pinyin" in the West. The pinyin alphabet is made up of 25 letters that are similar to English letters. It more closely represents the true sound of Chinese words than the old Wade-Giles system, which it has replaced for most English speakers. For example, Peking, the Wade-Giles spelling of China's capital city, is now Beijing, and the port city once known as Canton is Guangzhou.

When reading Chinese words, you should be aware of the pronounciation of these basic pinyin spellings:

c	is pronounced like ts in the English word tsar
z	is pronounced like dz or tz as in blitz
zh	is pronounced like j in job
q	is pronounced like ch in chin
x	is pronounced like sh in sheep
ui	is pronounced like w in way
i	is pronounced like ee in seen
a	is pronounced like ah in father
o	is pronounced like oo in look
shi	is pronounced like shur

However, certain Wade Giles spellings have become so familiar in English that they continue to be used. They include Hong Kong, the ancient city of Chang'an, and the Yangzi River. These "old fashioned" spellings are used in this book.

Just for fun, here are some useful Chinese words: ni hao (nee how) means hello; qing (cheeng) means please; xie xie (she eh she eh) means thank you, and zai jian (tzigh jee in) means goodbye.

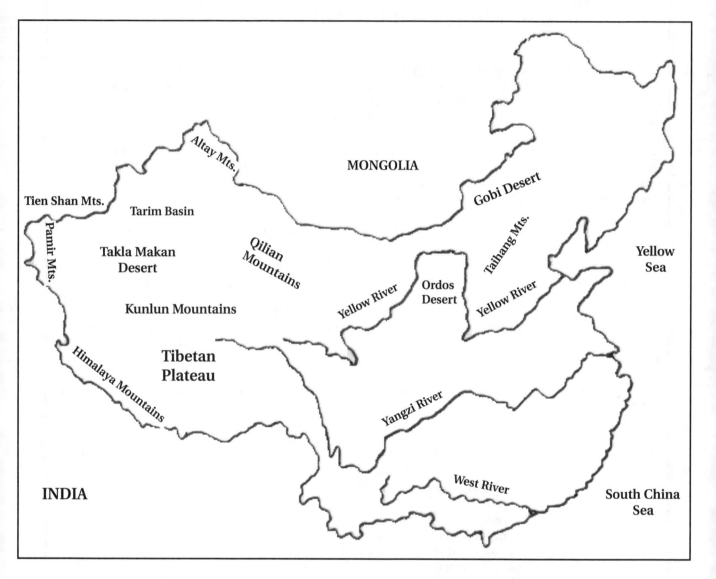

THE GEOGRAPHY OF CHINA

As you can see, the eastern part of China, known as "Inner China," is the most livable part of the country. It contains three major rivers — the Yellow, Yangzi, and West. This fertile region is surrounded by natural barriers. To the east is the ocean, to the north are mountains and the vast Gobi Desert, and to the west are more mountains and deserts. To the south of Inner China are steamy tropical forests that hindered settlement in ancient times. Today, China is divided into 21 provinces (22 counting Taiwan) and 5 autonomous regions.

CHAPTER 1

BEGINNINGS

(c. 7000 — 1750 BC)
THE CRADLE OF CHINESE CIVILIZATION

China is the third largest country in the world. Its 3 ¾ million square miles stretch from the barren wastelands of the subarctic to the lush rainforests of the tropics. Within its widely diverse landscape are many features of spectacular beauty — towering mountains, fertile river valleys, narrow gorges, and windswept plains. In fact, China holds a number of records in the world book of geography. Among these are the world's highest mountain (Mount Everest), the world's deepest and third longest river (the Yangzi), the world's largest and highest dry plateau (the Tibetan plateau), and the world's second largest desert (the Gobi).

Inner China

The eastern third of China is a fertile farming region. This is the heartland of the country, where most of the people live and work today. It is known as Inner China. Three major rivers flow eastward through this region and empty into the sea. From north to south, they are the Yellow River, the Yangzi River, and the West River. Much of China's history has centered in the valleys of these rivers. Find them on the map on the opposite page.

Because Inner China was surrounded by vast oceans, sizzling deserts, and rugged mountain ranges, the civilization that sprang up there was for a long time isolated from the rest of the world. This helps explain why the ancient Chinese called their homeland the Middle Kingdom and considered it the center of the earth.

The Yellow River

Chinese civilization began in the eastern valley of the Yellow River. The river flows through nearly 3,000 miles of widely varying landscape. Beginning in the moun-

---

Highlights of this Chapter

The Geography of China
The First Chinese People
The Yangshao Culture
The Longshan Culture
The Xia
China's Mythical Past

tains of the Tibetan plateau, it snakes eastward, making a big loop through the Gobi Desert and finally entering the North China Plain (of Inner China). Here it slows its pace, spreading out between banks as much as a mile apart before emptying into the sea.

The Yellow River's name is derived from the high content of silt it carries across the plain. The silt, which is called loess, is a type of yellowish-brown soil composed largely of ground-up limestone. At the end of the last Ice Age (about 20,000 years ago), heavy winds blew the loess from the Gobi Desert to the North China Plain. Most of it is still there. Some deposits of the loess are as deep as 200 feet! The yellow soil erodes easily, and in many places huge hills of loess end abruptly in steep cliffs. (People still live in dwellings hollowed out of the cliff faces.)

When it rains, some of the loess is washed away and carried by streams and tributaries into the river, turning it the dramatic shade of yellow that gives it is name. As the river proceeds to the sea, much of the loess settles to the bottom. Over the centuries, this has caused the riverbed to rise; in most parts the river is so shallow that only small boats can navigate. Occasionally the water level rises higher than the surrounding land, spilling over its banks and causing terrible floods. Since very early times, the Chinese have built dikes to keep the river within its banks, but the dikes occasionally break, allowing the river to run wild. The floods have caused the deaths of so many millions of people throughout history that the Yellow River is also known as *China's Sorrow.* The only benefit of the floods is the layer of loess that is deposited upon the floodplain, providing a natural fertilizer for the farmers' fields.

Sometimes the river changes course, cutting a new channel on its final lap to the sea. Between 602 BC and 1938 AD, it has flooded its banks 1,590 times and changed its course 26 times. The loess even gives the ocean water a yellowish tint, which is why this part of the Pacific Ocean is called the Yellow Sea.

The first farmers in China assumed that all soil was yellow, and they associated that color with fertility. In later years, yellow became the imperial color.

The Yangzi River

The Yangzi is China's longest river. It stretches for 3,494 miles. (Its name actually means "long river.") The source of the Yangzi is not terribly far from that of the

---

Loess has the consistency of flour, with granules so fine that if you were to rub some between your fingers they would disappear into the pores of your skin. And yet, this yellow soil is so firm that it can support a wall more than 100 feet high.

Yellow in the Tibetan plateau, as you can see in the map on page iv. From there, the Yangzi flows down through deep gulleys and canyons until it enters a hilly upland known as the Sichuan Basin. Over 700 tributaries flow into the Yangzi, giving it a much greater volume of water than the Yellow River. To the east of Sichuan the river passes through a series of magnificent gorges with sheer cliffs rising a thousand or more feet. Here the water grows turbulent and the river reaches its greatest depth of over 600 feet.

Beyond the gorges the Yangzi enters the scenic Lake Region of Inner China. This area receives a much greater rainfall than the arid north — nearly 60 inches each year! Lotus plants grow in abundance in the shallow lakes that line the Yangzi, and thousands of elegant Japanese cranes migrate to this tropical paradise each year. From the Lake Region the river fans out into a huge delta and then empties into the East China Sea.

The First Chinese People

Early humans probably first appeared in China over a million years ago. The earliest archaeological record of prehistoric man in China is known as Peking man, who lived about 400,000 years ago. His partial remains were discovered in 1927 in a limestone cave about 30 miles southwest of Beijing. (Peking is the Wade-Giles spelling of Beijing). Since then, many more remains have been found in eastern China. Peking man was an apelike fellow, who walked erect. (His species was *Homo Erectus*.) He stood about 5 feet tall. He had a big brow ridges, powerful jaws, large teeth, and a brain about 2/3 the capacity of a modern human. He made simple stone tools, knew how to make fires, and hunted wild animals, particularly deer, for food. Scientists believe that this line of early humans eventually died out without leaving direct descendants.

True humans, the direct ancestors of modern man (*Homo Sapiens Sapiens*), probably migrated to China from western Asia around 10,000 BC. They hunted wild prey with stone-tipped spears and gathered whatever nuts and seeds they could find. Archaeologists have discovered stone tools made by early humans dating back 15,000 years in scattered sites along the Yellow and Yangzi rivers.

Beginnings of Civilization

By 6,000 BC, some of the hunter-gatherers had learned how to plant the seeds of wild grasses. This was the first step in agriculture (farming) and marks the beginning of the Neolithic period. How did the people learn about farming? Most likely by accident. The women were in charge of gathering seeds, and one of them might have spilled some seeds into some moist soil. Suppose this happened just outside her hut. A few days later she would have noticed small plants poking their way out of the soil where she had spilled the seeds. If she was clever, she would have made the connection between the seeds and the plants. This sort of scenario probably occurred in many places in Inner China about this time. Pretty soon groups of families were planting their own crops. They had to settle down in permanent villages to tend them. This marked the end of their nomadic lifestyle and the very beginning of civilization.

In time, there were many villages in the river valleys. The farmers in the Yellow River valley grew millet (a grain something like wheat), while those living further south learned to grow rice. Rice farming required more labor. The rice seeds were sewn in dry land, and as soon as the seedlings were a few inches tall they were transplanted in large pools of shallow water called paddies.

The farmers stored their grain in pots, which they made from clay collected along the river bed. It didn't take them long to discover that firing (baking) the pots in a hot oven made of rocks produced a harder and more durable surface. Once fired, these containers were fairly sturdy, and they could be used for cooking food over a fire.

From earliest times, the people of the river valley had tamed dogs, the descendants of wolves, and during the Neolithic period many families kept these animals as home protectors and hunting companions. The farmers also tamed wild pigs and raised them in pens. Pigs became a prime source of meat in China, since they were easy to feed and they didn't require much room.

By working together, the farmers were able to produce more food than they needed. This freed up certain members of the group to perform other tasks, such as making new tools for the community. This specialization of tasks is an important stage of development in a civilization.

Over the centuries, many distinctive cultures evolved in Inner China. Among these, two stand out for their artistic styles and burial practices. These were the Yangshao and the Longshan. Let's take a closer look.

The Yangshao

The Yangshao (Yawng show) culture flourished from 5000 to 3000 BC along the valleys of the central Yellow River and the Wei River (a major tributary of the Yellow River). We know a great deal about these people because over 1,000 widely scattered sites have been discovered and closely studied by archaeologists. The richest site is an

The oldest rice grains in the world, dating from 5000 BC, were found baked into pottery in marshland near the mouth of the Yangzi.

early Yangshao village discovered in the 1950's at Banpo (near Xi'an in present-day Shanxi province).

The people of Banpo lived in round, single room huts made of wooden poles, the walls plastered with mud. The foundations of the huts were dug about a foot below the surface of the ground to insulate them from the summer heat and the winter cold. The roofs were covered with thatch (bunches of dried grasses tied together and arranged in layers). Each hut was a cozy dwelling, with a hearth in the center for heat and cooking. Wide benches built into the walls were used for sleeping.

Banpo was made up of 46 of these huts, as well as a few larger square structures, which were probably used for meetings and ceremonies. Scattered among the dwellings were animal enclosures for pigs and six kilns (ovens for firing pottery).

Many of the reddish pots that have been discovered at the Banpo site are decorated with geometric designs — spirals, diamonds, and zigzags — painted on with a mixture of minerals and water. Other pots are decorated with human faces and animals — fish, cranes, and deer. (The animals depicted give us a good idea of what the villagers ate for dinner.) There are even symbols that might be a primitive form of writing. These paintings are among the oldest examples of Chinese art.

The village itself was surrounded by a

Banpo meeting house

deep ditch, no doubt for defensive purposes. Beyond this was a cemetery with 200 simple graves. The Banpo people apparently believed in an afterlife, because they buried their dead with utensils and even food.

The Longshan

The Longshan (Lung shan) culture began in the Yellow River basin around 3000 BC and spread throughout much of Inner China. Longshan dwellings were made of earth that had been firmly packed and coated with chalk. Defensive walls of packed earth surrounded the villages. The Longshan were more warlike than the Yangshao, and there is evidence that they sacrificed humans during religious rituals.

The Longshan were the first people to use a potter's wheel. This simple device enabled them to make finer ceramic (clay) pieces than those of the Yangshao. Their most distinctive ceramics were elegant black vases that had a shiny black surface. These were made with an iron-rich clay that turned black from the smoke and high temperatures when they were fired in sealed kilns. Some were nearly as thin as an eggshell. The shiny vessels were probably used for religious ceremonies.

Pots for everyday use were shaped by hand and fired at a lower temperature. Many of the cups and bowls stood on a circular foot. Thicker-walled pots rested upon a tripod (three "feet"), so that they could be placed among the embers of the fire to heat the liquids they contained. Some pots had spouts, handles, and lids.

Longshan craftsmen also worked with jade, a very hard stone formed from the crystals of rocks that have been crushed over millions of years. Jade was not easily molded. The craftsman had to patiently grind it down using a paste made of sand and grease and a stone or copper tool. His labor was worth the effort, since the finished product was practically indestructible. The Longshan made jade figurines of animals and birds as well as pendants.

Round jade discs (*bi*), hollowed out in the center (imagine the effort required to do that!), were used during ritual sacrifices.

Unlike the Yangshao, the Longshan buried their dead in wooden coffins within their settlement walls, often under the floors of their houses. We know that there were clear social distinctions in their society because the larger graves contained luxury objects like jade figures and shiny black vases, while the smaller graves held just a few ordinary pots and tools.

The Xia

Around 1900 BC, the first known city in China was founded at Erlitou, along the Yellow River. The beginnings of a true civilization were beginning to emerge in China. A civilized society has a well-defined class structure, a large-scale military force, and a system of government that rules a population living in a large territory from a central "capital." Erlitou was one of the capitals of a kingdom ruled by the Xia (Shee yah), China's first dynasty. (A dynasty is a family of rulers in which power is passed down from generation to generation, usually from father to son.)

For a long time, archaeologists were

As early as 3000 BC rice farmers were using water buffalos to help them plow their fields and harvest the grain. Although they can be obstinate, water buffalos (called oxen in the north) love to be in the mud and water, and they were able to pull plows through rice paddies where the water was up to their knees.

not certain that the Xia existed at all. Although there were many legends about them, no hard evidence had turned up. The situation changed in 1959 with the discovery at Erlitou of the foundations of a palace covering about 110,000 square feet, as well as a series of tombs.

A wealth of artifacts found at the site included a primitive plow, pottery, and pieces of carved jade. Most exciting was the discovery of the earliest bronze objects known to exist. Bronze is a hard metal produced by melting copper and tin together. Early craftsmen probably figured out how to smelt metal ore (melt it down) after using the high-temperature kilns to fire ceramic pots.

Most of the bronze articles found at Erlitou were simple tools, like fishhooks and awls, as well as weapons — edged daggers and arrowheads. These were made by hammering chunks of the hardened metal. More impressive were the bronze containers, whose tripod shapes resembled pieces of Longshan pottery. These vessels were made by pouring liquid bronze into clay molds. They were apparently used for religious ceremonies as containers for food offerings to the spirits or for a beverage that was consumed during a ritual.

Based upon the great size of the palace at Erlitou and the artifacts found there and in the nearby gravesites, we know that the Xia were an advanced society with distinct class divisions. Although most people were ordinary farmers, there was a small middle class of craftsmen and an upper class of warriors. The Xia ruler was also the chief priest. He led ritual ceremonies and even sacrificed human beings to appease a variety of nature gods.

China's Legendary Past

Everything else we know about the Xia rulers comes from the ancient legends. China's earliest "history" was, in fact, a blend of fact and fantasy created by storytellers. This "pseudo-history" of the time before there is actual evidence of Chinese culture and the colorful tales of early mythical rulers were accepted and revered as part of China's national heritage until very recent times.

Let's put aside the purely historical records for the moment and see how the Chinese storytellers explained the creation of their civilization.

The Cosmic Egg

In the beginning, so the story goes, all the elements of the world mingled in the darkness within a giant egg. These scrambled elements were parts of the two major forces of the universe, known as *yin* and *yang*. One day the elements burst through the shell of the egg. The heavier ones, which made up *yin*, sank and formed the earth, while the lighter ones, which made up *yang*, floated up, forming the sky. Suddenly, between the earth and sky, appeared a strange-looking dwarf called Pangu. His body was covered with hair; he had two horns thrusting from his forehead and two tusks from his upper jaw. As the sky separated from the earth, Pangu grew and grew so that he could keep them apart. Finally, after 18,000 years, the sky and earth were fixed in their permanent positions. Then, exhausted, Pangu died.

The parts of Pangu's body became different features of the natural world. His head became the sacred mountain of the north, his stomach became the center of the (flat) earth, his left arm the sacred mountain of the south, his right arm the sacred mountain of the east, and his feet the sacred mountain of the west.

Pangu's breath turned into the mist, clouds, and winds, and his sweat became the rain. His voice boomed across the land as thunder. His eyes became the sun and moon, and his beard became the stars. And there was more. His blood was transformed into the rivers, his flesh became the soil, his hair bloomed into plants and trees, his teeth and bones hardened into minerals, and the marrow in his bones crystallized into pearls and precious gems. The fleas that had lived in the giant's body were blown across all creation — they became the people.

As you can see, the tortoise of Chinese mythology had a more fanciful appearance than his more natural cousin. He was a symbol of strength, endurance, and longevity. The tortoise was also thought to be a model of the world. Its upper shell was curved like the heavens, and the lower shell was flat, the way the ancient Chinese believed the earth to be.

Some stories described how Pangu was helped in his labors by four beasts, which emerged with him from the cosmic egg. These were the dragon, the phoenix, the unicorn, and the tortoise. (See the figure above.) They later produced others of their own kind. These four creatures would play a major role in Chinese mythology and religious beliefs.

The ancient Chinese believed the sacred mountains held the heavens up from the earth.

The Three Sovereigns

Once the world was formed and people were living on it, there began an era of superhuman kings. They gave the Chinese people everything they needed to create a great civilization.

The first three came to be known as the Three Sovereigns. Fuxi (foo shee), the Ox Tamer, taught people how to tame animals, gave them nets for hunting and fishing, and invented music and musical instruments. Shennong, the Divine Farmer, invented the plow and the hoe. He taught the people how to farm and market products and how to use plant remedies for medicine. Legend says that he tried every possible herb concoction to determine its medicinal value or toxicity. (It's a good thing he was superhuman!)

Huangdi (huh wang dee), "the Yellow Emperor," invented the bow and arrow, boats and carts, the potter's wheel, the calendar, and handwriting. He fought a great battle against enemy tribesmen, securing the Yellow River valley for his people. (This explains why he was called the Yellow Emperor.)

The Three Sages

Huangdi was also the founder of a second sequence of legendary rulers. Many tales were told about these mighty warriors, who were constantly at war with the forces of evil — battling floods, fighting monsters, and heroically striving to better the lives of the Chinese people. The last three — Yao, Shun, and Yu — were most highly revered. They were known as the Three Sages (Wise Men). Yao (yow) taught the people about the arts and religious rituals. When he grew old, he decided not to hand over power to his unworthy son; instead, he chose Shun, a poor peasant, to succeed him. (In later centuries, the philosopher Confucius would admire Shun, because he believed that personal merit rather than hereditary should determine who should rule.)

Shun turned out to be a good ruler. When the river flooded its banks, he assigned to an official named Yu (you) the task of controlling the water. Yu built channels and drained the water out to sea, so the farmers could return to their fields. (Flooding, as you know, was a big problem in China.)

Yu became Shun's successor. He founded the kingdom of Xia and united

---

Have you noticed that the number three appears often in Chinese mythology? Three was considered a lucky and magical number. When it was multiplied by itself, it produced nine — a number so highly regarded it was associated with the emperor. See how many times these numbers (three and nine) appear in our story about ancient China.

most of northern China under his rule. He divided China into nine provinces. Ores from each province were used to make nine tripod cauldrons. These cauldrons became important symbols of imperial power. They were passed down from ruler to ruler. Remember the cauldrons. You'll be hearing more about them in Chapter 5.

When Yu died, the people ignored the successor he had chosen and turned to Yu's son to lead them. In this way, they showed their preference for a hereditary transfer of power. Yu and his son were the first two kings of China's first dynasty, the Xia. This is where legend ends and "real" history begins.

The Fall of the Xia

The Xia are believed to have had 17 rulers. They reigned for almost 500 years. The last ruler, Jie, was a cruel tyrant, who used his position to cater to his own pleasure. He allegedly set tigers from the royal zoo free in a marketplace for the fun of watching the people run for their lives!

Jie was so hated that when Li, the Lord of Shang (Shawng), led a revolt against him, people flocked to join his (Li's) cause. Li and his followers overthrew Jia in 1751 BC. The defeated king fled south, where he lived out his last years in impoverished exile, pining for his lost powers. So ended the mighty Xia dynasty.

In the centuries that followed the overthrow of Jie, the Chinese began keeping written records of important events. The ancient myths and legends you've been reading about gradually merged with recorded history so that, in time, the living ruler of China could trace his lineage all the way back to the mythical Yellow Emperor.

Review Questions

1. What three major rivers flow through Inner China?

2. What is loess?

3. In what major way does the Yangzi differ from the Yellow River?

4. What marks the beginning of the Neolithic Period?

5. Describe the village of Banpo.

6. Compare the pots of the Longshan and the Yangshao.

7. How was bronze made?

8. What were the class divisions in Xia society?

9. What were the *yin* and *yang*?

10. Who was Pangu, and what did he do for 18,000 years?

11. Who was the Yellow Emperor?

12. What were the nine caldrons?

13. Who were (supposedly) the first two rulers of the Xia?

14. Who led the revolt against the last Xia ruler?

Projects

1. In an atlas, find a map of modern China that shows the 21 provinces and 5 autonomous regions. Choose one of the provinces and find out about its climate and geography. Write several paragraphs to describe them. Then draw a map of the province. Paste the map and paragraph on a piece of posterboard. Add other illustrations if you can. Share your poster with your classmates.

2. Look in your library or on the Internet for more information about the Neolithic period in China. Then find out about the same period in Mesopotamia. Make a chart comparing the Neolithic cultures in these two parts of the world.

3. Most ancient civilizations were founded in river valleys. (For example, think of Egypt, Sumer, Rome, and the valley of the Indus River.) Why do you think this is true? Write a paragraph explaining your views about this.

4. Using clay dough made of flour, water, and salt and a thick piece of cardboard, make a relief map of Inner China. Paint the major rivers and the ocean in blue, the Yellow River valley yellow, and the Yangzi valley green.

5. Using clay, toothpicks, and whatever other materials are available, make a model of Banpo on a sheet of cardboard.

6. Make a clay model of a tripod. When it's dry, decorate it as you think a Longshan potter might have done.

7. The discovery of the site of the Xia palace at Erlitou is much like that of ancient Troy. Both were considered mythical places until their ruins were discovered. Both sites actually consisted of many cities, built one upon another over a long period of time. There were four layers (cities) at Erlitou, dating from 2010 to 1324 2010 BC. Troy had nine layers. Find out more about ancient Troy and Erlitou. Then make a poster comparing and contrasting these two archaeological sites.

8. Draw a picture of Pangu, or make a model of him out of clay.

9. Write a poem about the Chinese myth of creation.

10. Consult a book in your library about the mythical rulers of China that were mentioned in this chapter. Then make a chart, listing their names and major contributions to Chinese culture.

11. Make a timeline of the major events (the historical ones) and achievements covered in this chapter.

Happenings Elsewhere in the Ancient World

Old Kingdom in ancient Egypt (3100-2160 BC)

Rise of Sumerian civilization in Mesopotamia (c 3000 BC)

First cities in the Indus Valley (c 2500 BC)

Farming villages flourishing in Peru (c 2000 BC)

Beginnings of Minoan culture on island of Crete (c 1700 BC)

CHAPTER 2
THE SHANG DYNASTY

(1750 — 1027 BC)
BONES AND BRONZES

After Li, the Lord of Shang defeated the Xia, he established his own new dynasty — the Shang. Thirty Shang kings would rule for nearly 700 years. Because many examples of writing have been discovered in sites dating from this period, the Shang dynasty marks the beginning of recorded history in China.

Organizing the Kingdom

When he became king, Li took the name of Tang the Victorious. (We'll refer to him as Tang.) Throughout Chinese history, each new ruler would follow this tradition of choosing a special "throne name."

Tang had a big job ahead of him. His first task was to unify his kingdom. He left the local tribal chiefs in control of their territories, requiring only that they come to court at given intervals to present gifts to him as a token of their loyalty. (This is known as paying tribute.) He granted other tracts of land to his relatives and main followers, in exchange for their loyalty and military support. These men formed a new class of nobles. They built walled towns, which resembled fortresses, and defended their land with their own private armies. The kingdom was thus divided into smaller parts that were ruled by men the king felt he could depend upon.

Tang appointed special officials to perform such functions as collecting taxes and overseeing his building projects. He traveled constantly around his realm to keep in close touch with the nobles and tribal chiefs and to remind everyone that he was in charge.

Over the years, the Shang kings expanded their territory until they ruled most of the northern and central parts of Inner China. As the kingdom grew, the larger towns became cities. At the peak of Shang

Highlights of This Chapter

The Shang Government and Army
The Chinese Dragon
The Oracle Bones
The Chinese Calendar
Early Porcelain
Bronze Vessels
The Production of Silk
The Shang Tombs

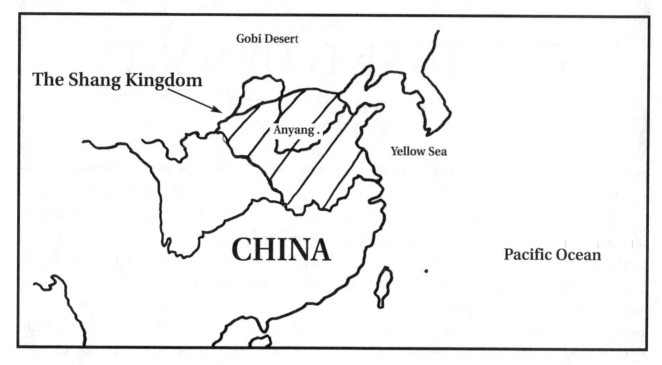

The Shang Kingdom

Gobi Desert

Anyang .

CHINA

Yellow Sea

Pacific Ocean

power there were over 1,000 walled cities.

People living on the edges of the kingdom were considered barbarians. They were often captured on raids to become slaves or human sacrifices for the Shang gods.

The Shang Army

These were violent times. Although the nobles acknowledged the authority of the king, they often fought among themselves over land ownership. And whenever the barbarians organized an assault against the borders, the king led his army to drive them back.

The typical campaign army had between 3,000 and 5,000 men. While the common soldiers marched on foot, the nobles fought from chariots that had spoked wheels. These were the first wheeled vehicles in China. The chariots were usually drawn by two horses. The Shang obtained the horses in Mongolia. The animals were highly valued on the battlefield, and no one would have dreamed of hitching one up to a farmer's plow!

Shang warriors carried weapons made of bronze — daggers, spear points and arrow heads, and halberds. (A halberd was a long-handled weapon carried by a

Chariots were also used in royal hunts for deer, bears, tigers, wild boar, elephants, and rhinoceroses. The fact that these animals were abundant tells us that much of the north China plain was heavily forested in those early times. Today the trees are few and far between in this region.

foot soldier. It had an axe-like blade on one end.) The nobles wore bronze helmets and armor made of ox or rhinoceros hide.

The City of Anyang

The Shang moved their capital several times, as the local resources (metal ores, wood, and soil) became exhausted. The ruins of Anyang, the last capital, were discovered in 1928. Excavations of the royal tombs at Anyang have yielded thousands of artifacts that tell us much about the lives of the Shang ruling class.

Archaeologists were amazed by the precise manner in which Anyang was laid out. It covered an area of nine square miles (three miles on each side). From what remains, we can tell that the king lived and worked in an imposing wooden palace in the heart of the city. It was surrounded by large gardens. Outside the palace complex were temples and the homes of the nobles and government officials. The buildings were rectangular, and the important ones had south-facing entrances. The city streets formed a grid, running north-south and east-west and intersecting at neat right angles.

Anyang was surrounded by a massive rectangular wall made of layers of "rammed earth" — dirt that was packed so tightly it formed a solid, inpenetrable mass. The city was entered through a large gatehouse in the southern part of the wall. Just outside the wall were the workshops of craftsmen, the homes of commoners, and the burial grounds.

This city plan — with its grid of streets, rectangular wooden buildings facing south, and protective earthen wall — would be the basic design of nearly all Chinese cities until modern times.

Life On The Farm

Throughout Chinese history, most of the people have been farmers. This is true even today. In Shang times, the farmers worked for the king as well as for themselves. They owed the king a certain amount of labor (such as building city walls and tombs) as well as a stint in the army. They also paid taxes. There was no money; they paid in sacks of grain.

The farmers lived in villages and worked together in the fields. Those living near the rivers dug irrigation canals to

---

The number nine was considered very lucky. Perhaps this was because it was the largest single digit, and it could be neatly divided into three parts. (Three was also a lucky number, but not as lucky as nine!) Nine would later become the imperial number, just as yellow would be the imperial color. Throughout this book you'll be running into many examples of objects, concepts, and even people arranged in groups of three or nine. Be on the lookout for them!

transport water to their fields. They also built dikes for flood control.

Traders from western Asia brought wheat to China in about 1200 BC, and it quickly replaced millet as the main crop grown in the Yellow River valley. The wheat was ground into flour, which was used to make noodles. These noodles became as important to the menu of northern China as rice was further south. The flour was also the main ingredient of dumplings, which were often stuffed with garlic and onions and then steamed over a hot fire.

The Shang were the first people in China to eat soybeans. These were brought to the Yellow River valley from Manchuria, a region to the northeast. The soybean is in the same family as peas. (Both are legumes.) Soybeans are amazingly nutritious. They contain more protein than any other plant or animal food. The Chinese dried the soybean seeds and then crushed them to extract the oil, which they used for cooking. What remained of the seed was used to make soy sauce. Soybeans were easy to grow and store, and they would prove to be a crucial food source in times of famine.

The Power of the Spirits

Like most primitive people, the Shang believed that good and bad spirits inhabited every aspect of nature. These spirits were said to live in rocks, trees, streams, mountains, rivers, and the sea. The greatest of all the spirits was the high god, Shangdi. (His name literally means "the Shang god.") The people built stone altars and placed food and wine there for Shangdi and the other spirits, offering prayers for their support. They feared that a failure to honor the deities would result in such disasters as a poor harvest, a flood, or a loss in battle.

As with the Xia, the Shang king was the chief priest. At moments of great crisis, he sacrificed human beings to Shangdi, sometimes dozens at a time.

The Friendly Dragon

The dragon has always been an important figure in Chinese culture. But unlike the fierce, man-eating monster of European mythology, the Chinese dragon is a benevolent creature.

The ancient Chinese considered the dragon a sort of king of all the scaly creatures — fish, lizards, and snakes — who were known to live in dark, wet places. In time, a series of myths evolved about the powerful (but kindly) dragons that lived in the ocean and rivers. It was said that when the tides came in, the dragons were surfacing. When the tides when out, the thirsty dragons were taking a long drink.

Dragons had wings, and in the spring, according to the ancient beliefs, they flew up into the clouds and produced gentle rain to water the farmers' crops.

Thunder was caused by their frolicking in the sky. In autumn, the dragons returned to the rivers and seas. They stayed there all winter (a cold, dry season in the Yellow River valley), dwelling in crystal palaces that were filled with pearls and precious gems.

The dragon's appearance was rather fanciful. The earliest myths described a serpent-like animal with fish scales and a long beard. As time went on, the dragon acquired other featuress — the head of a camel, the whiskers of a cat, the antlers of a deer, the ears of a bull, the throat of a snake, the mane of a horse, and the claws of an eagle. It also had the gleaming eyes of a demon, and it was known to breathe fire.

Special ceremonies were performed in the spring to please the dragons so that they would provide plenty of rain for the crops. Dragons were said to be fond of roasted swallows, so these birds were often sacrificed on special altars.In the fall, the farmers thanked the dragons for the bounty of their harvest.

The Oracle Bones

The Shang believed that the spirits of their dead ancestors also lived in the heavens, and that they influenced the fortunes of the living. The kings always sought the advice of these spirits before making important decisions. They believed the spirits revealed the answers to their questions through the patterns of cracks produced by heating animal bones and the undersides of tortoise shells.

Using such methods to predict the future is called divination. Here's how it worked. The king presented a question about such matters as his chances in an upcoming military campaign or the meaning of a dream to a diviner (a priest who interpreted signs about the future). The diviner then scraped long furrows on a flat, polished piece of bone, usually the shoulder bone of an ox. Then he applied a heated metal bar to the back of the bone. The heat produced a pattern of cracks in the bone, which were believed to be the ancestors' reply to the king's question. The diviner interpreted the cracks and then carved these answers onto the bone. He used simple picture-writing (symbols of the sun, animals, plants, and other common facets of nature). Over 150,000 fragments of these "oracle bones" have been found in the sites of ancient Shang cities.

The practice of divining the future from the cracks on bones dates back to Neolithic times, but it was not until the Shang era that the answers (and sometimes the questions) were recorded on the bones. The picture-writing symbols are called characters. Over 3,000 appear on the oracle bones that have been studied. Of the thousand that have been deciphered so far, some represent a specific thing (like a tree) and others seem to represent sounds

Because of the large number of symbols used on the bones, historians suspect that a written language had existed in China for quite a long time. However, the Shang inscriptions are the first known examples of written Chinese texts, and they provide us with many interesting glimpses of the lives of the Shang. Many of the characters used today can be traced back to those carved on the oracle bones.

Sky Watching

As you might expect, the people who lived in very ancient times were terrified by such unusual events as an eclipse of the sun or moon, or the sudden appearance of a comet. Because the Shang farmers didn't understand why these things happened, they assumed them to be omens or messages from the spirits. But what was their meaning? Since the king was the chief priest

Before discoveries of large collections of oracle bones by archaeologists in the 19th century, similar bones, known in Chinese society of that time as "dragon bones," had been dug up and then ground up for medicine. The people thought the inscriptions gave the bones magical powers. Fortunately, with the new discovery, the bones have been recognized for what they are.

and their major link with the spirits, they reasoned that he should be able to explain and even predict these unsettling occurrences.

So the kings appointed groups of men to study the heavens. Every night, these sky watchers went out to the city walls to observe and record what they saw. They made detailed maps of the celestial bodies and noted that the changing seasons were marked by the apparent movement of the stars. They learned to recognize patterns and could even make certain predictions.

As early as 1300 BC, royal astronomers were recording eclipses of the sun and moon as well as the movements of comets. (Some of these records have been found on fragments of oracle bones) The astronomers learned to calculate eclipses of the moon in advance so accurately that the king came to depend upon their predictions, and an error of 24 hours was a cause for alarm. The astronomers were so skillful

they were given the duty of keeping other records. They became China's first historians.

The royal astronomers used their observations of the moon to create a calendar, which provided guidelines for the farmers as to when to plant and harvest their crops. A week was made up of ten days. Three weeks made a month, six weeks (two months) made a "cycle" of 60 days, and six cycles made a year of 360 days. When it became obvious that the calendar was not totally "in synch" with the solar year, the astronomers tried adding extra days at the end of the year. It didn't take them long to realize that five (and sometimes six) was the "magic number." Certain days of the year were considered lucky or unlucky. The Shang calendar with its ten-day weeks and 60-day cycles appears in inscriptions on the oracle bones. And it is similar to the one used in modern China.

Thanks to the skills of the royal

The Shang were certainly not the first people in China to observe the heavens. In about 3000 BC earlier astronomers carved a detailed chart of the heavens in stone. They represented groups of stars as circles linked with lines. Like the constellations familiar to westerners, these shapes resembled animals, and there was even a big dipper. By 2000 BC Chinese astronomers had defined and named 28 constellations along the sun's apparent path through the stars.

The Dragon constellation appeared in the eastern night sky beginning in March. It was probably because of this that the Dragon came to be associated with spring and the east. (Of course, the east was also the direction the rain usually came from.) The Tiger constellation was most apparent in the western sky in autumn and was linked with that season and direction. The other seasons and directions were represented by the phoenix bird (summer and the south) and the tortoise (winter and the north).

astronomers, the Shang king could accurately predict unusual happenings in the heavens. As for explaining the meanings of these happenings, the king counted upon the ingenuity of his priests and diviners. Usually they were interpreted as ominous forbodings of doom. For example, the appearance of a comet came to be regarded as a bad omen for the government, and the conjunction of planets (planets appearing to come together in outer space) signified that the ruling dynasty was in danger of collapse. Remember this. Before long, you will be hearing about the occurence of one of these bad omens.

Early Porcelain

The very earliest porcelain was made during the Shang dynasty. Porcelain is a type of pottery with a hard, shiny glaze. Because the pieces made by Shang potters were relatively primitive compared to those made in later centuries, experts refer to them as "proto-porcelain."

Like so many important discoveries, the process of glazing was most likely discovered by accident. Someone must have noticed that if bits of airborn soot happened to land on a clay pot while it was being fired in a kiln, shiny patches would appear. After noting this, the next logical step was to intentionally brush bits of ash onto a pot before firing it. At a temperature of more than 1,200 C., the ash would melt and form a glassy coating over the entire surface. An object finished in this way would be not only attractive but very hard and resistant to breakage.

The Shang potters became rather adept at making delicate cups and vases of "proto-porcelain." They used kaolin, a fine white clay found in many parts of Inner China.

Bronze Vessels

The bowls and goblets made by the Shang bronzesmiths were of far higher quality than those of the Xia. In fact, many art historians argue that the technique of the Shang bronzesmiths and the beauty of their creations have *never* been surpassed in China or elsewhere.

To make a bronze vessel, the craftsman first made a clay model and fired it. He then pressed hunks of clay around the model to make a set of four molds. Next he worked another hunk of clay into the basic shape of the model, only smaller. This formed an inner core mold. The next step was to arrange the four outer molds around the inner core mold on a flat piece of wet clay. When the base was dry and the pieces were firmly attached, the craftsman poured a molten mixture of bronze — nine parts copper and one part tin — into the thin space between the outer mold and inner core.

After the bronze cooled and solidified, the clay molds were broken apart and removed. What remained was a handsome metal vessel resembling the original clay model. The craftsman cast extra parts — like legs, handles, spouts, and lids — separately and then soldered them on.

The final step was to carve figures of animals, birds, plants, and geometric designs (especially spirals) onto the vessel. (Sometimes, figures were cut into the inner parts of the molds; these would stand out in relief (raised above the surface) on the bronze piece.) Many Shang vessels featured a monster face (a *taotie*), which was perhaps intended to chase away evil spirits. And, as you might expect, there were plenty of dragons.

Inscriptions found *inside* many of the bronze sacrificial vessels are fine examples of early Chinese writing. They marked major dates and events, or simply expressed such wishes as "May sons and grandsons for a myriad years cherish and use this cup."

Many of the smaller tripod (three-legged) vessels were intended for heating wine, which was made from fermented rice. Wine was consumed in great quantities by the king and nobles during religious ceremonies. It produced a euphoric, relaxed state of mind, which heightened the sense of the presence of the spirits. (In later centuries, certain historians scoffed at the Shang noblemen, referring to them as drunkards because of the great amount of

A Tripod

wine they consumed!) Some containers were incredibly big. A huge cauldron was found that weighs over 400 pounds! (It is the largest bronze object ever unearthed in China.) The bronze vessels themselves were regarded as sacred objects, since they had been "magically" transformed from molten metal into solid objects.

The fact that thousands of vessels have survived gives us a good idea of how important the bronze industry was in Shang society. Just imagine the great management skills required of the king and his government officials to mobilize the men and material to mine, transport, and refine the copper and tin ores, to manufacture the clay models, cores, and molds used in the casting process, and to run the foundries where the vessels were produced. The bronze industry was "big business," a clear indicator of a complex, well-organized civilization.

The Production of Silk

Another important product of the Shang dynasty was silk. Silk cloth has ranked among the most treasured products of China for millennia. It is valued for its smooth texture, its sheer quality, and its shimmery colors when it is dyed. According to legend, Empress Xiling Shi (wife of the Yellow Emperor) discovered silk about 4,500 years ago. The emperor had asked her to find out what was wrong with the mulberry trees in his garden. She went to the garden and saw that the trees were covered with a mass of cocoons. She plucked a cocoon and dropped it into a pot of water. To her amazement, the cocoon softened into a tangled web that could be unraveled like a ball of yarn until there was a single, slender strand. The empress later made a reel to spin together several strands into silk thread, which she wove into the first piece of silk cloth.

Although this is just a legend, the secret of making silk was probably discovered in China in Neolithic times. By the Shang era, silk weavers were adept at producing fine fabric. One of the earliest surviving pieces of evidence of silk weaving is a Shang fragment, transmuted in the patina (surface covering) of a bronze vessel.

Shang women wove the silk by hand on a back loom. The weaver fastened the ends of the vertical (warp) threads to belts around her waist and held them tight with wooden bars under her feet. She was then able to pass the horizontal (weft) threads over and under the vertical warp threads.

Throughout history women managed every aspect of silk making. They raised the silkworms, plunged the cocoons into boiling water to loosen and separate the filaments before the adult moths could bite their way out, then carefully wound the strands onto reels.

Silk was a luxury item worn only by the very rich. Everyone else wore clothing made from the fibers of the hemp plant. Cotton, which was introduced from India in about the 6th century AD, later became the major fabric for everyday use.

Shang Burials

The Shang believed that after their kings and high nobles died, their souls would continue to enjoy the comforts they

Remember Jie, the last ruler of the Xia? His extravagance seems to have had no limit. One legend describes how, when he heard that his favorite concubine liked the sound of tearing silk, he ordered bale after bale to be shredded, for her entertainment!

had known in this world, as long as they were buried properly. Their bodies were placed in wooden coffins and buried with luxury items in vast tombs in the ground. Some archaeologists suggest that mourners at the funeral might have poured an offering of wine to the deceased and then tossed in the vessel as well. This would help explain the huge number of bronze cups in the tombs.

Many coffins were surrounded by human remains. It seems that wives, servants, and even soldiers willingly gave their lives at the time of the funeral so that they could serve their lord in the afterlife. Groups of slaves and prisoners of war died less willingly. Apparently their bodies were offered as a sacrifice to the gods. They were usually bound and then buried (often alive!) in pits dug just outside the tomb. One tomb complex at Anyang held the remains of 90 followers and 74 slaves and prisoners — as well as 12 horses and 11 dogs.

Do you remember how the city of Anyang was aligned with the four cardinal directions, with the streets meeting at right angles? Shang tombs mirrored this design. Four access ramps led down into the tomb, the main ones going north-south and the secondary ones east-west.

The royal tomb at Zhengzhou (another Shang capital) was huge. It was 60 feet wide, 40 feet deep, and 2,385 feet long. The Shang government had to mobilize thousands of workers to dig the pits and then fill them in again with tightly-packed earth.

The Tomb of Lady Hao

In 1976 archaeologists digging near Anyang unearthed the tomb of Lady Hao, favorite wife of the king, Wu Ding. This was the only Shang tomb never to have been disturbed at all before it was excavated. (It had been protected by the foundations of a temple Wu Ding built over it.) Although it was a fairly small tomb (13 by 18 feet wide and 25 feet deep), it was heaped with treasures. Among these were 460 bronze objects, including more than 130 weapons, 23 bells, 27 knives, 4 mirrors, and 4 statues of tigers. Sixty of the bronze vessels bore Lady Hao's name. There were also 755 jade objects, 70 stone sculptures, nearly 500 bone hairpins, over 20 bone arrowheads, and 3 ivory carvings. An ivory wine-cup was nearly a foot tall and inlaid with turquoise. Apart from these riches, there were nearly 7,000 cowrie shells, an ancient form of currency. The tomb also held 16 human skeletons.

Projects for the living also involved large numbers of laborers. The city wall of Zhengzhou — four miles long and 66 feet thick — would have taken 10,000 workers ten to twenty years to complete!

We know something about Lady Hao because she was mentioned in several oracle bone inscriptions. Wu Ding had asked the spirits many questions about her illnesses and pregnancies. We also know from the inscriptions that she was quite an adventurous woman. She owned a landed estate near Anyang and took charge of certain religious rituals (a role usually reserved for men). She even led several military campaigns; one against the Qiang tribesmen to the west involved 13,000 troops. (This accounts for all those weapons found in her tomb!)

Try to remember Lady Hao as you read on about the many dynasties of ancient China. Even though the government was run by powerful men, every once in a while an extraordinary woman did appear on the scene and take center stage. They were some of the greatest heroines — and villainesses — of the ancient world.

The Fall of the Shang

The last Shang kings were less able warriors than their predecessors. This put the kingdom at great risk when its borders were threatened by fierce tribesmen such as the Qiang (the very same "barbarians" who had once tangled with Lady Hao!). The later kings were not very competent rulers either, and many of their subjects began to grumble about their shortcomings. On May 28, 1059 BC, there was a spectacular conjunction of the five visible planets — Mercury, Venus, Mars, Jupiter, and Saturn. As you know, this was considered a sign that the present dynasty was coming to an end. The members of the royal household must have been biting their fingernails!

Stories were later told about the cruelty and wickedness of the last Shang king, Di Xin. Some said that he committed cruel acts to please his beautiful (but evil) wife, Dan Ji. (Di Xin sounds a lot like the last Xia ruler, doesn't he?) Of greater interest here is the story describing his dealings with King Wen of Zhou.

The Kingdom of Zhou was nestled in the Wei River valley between the Qiang and the Shang capital. The Zhou paid an annual tribute to the Shang. As the story goes, Di Xin arrested King Wen for failing to express what he considered the proper respect. The Shang king later captured Wen's son, then had him killed, boiled in a broth, and served to Wen! Di Xin laughed when he heard that his prisoner had consumed the stew, unaware of its content. When Wen later died in captivity, his heir, Wu, sought revenge for this inhumane act.

The incident of boiling the prince and serving him to his father is probably not true, but there is little doubt that the Zhou and the Shang came to blows. We know that during the last years of the Shang dynasty the Zhou grew so powerful that King Wen controlled nearly two-thirds of the Shang frontier territories. We also know that King Wen died as a prisoner of Di Xin, and that his eldest son, Wu, led a huge army against his former captors in an epic battle at Muye (near Anyang). The Zhou later took great joy in describing how the Shang soldiers lost heart against their superior forces and fled the battlefield.

The defeated Di Xin was said to have made his way back to his palace, where he dressed up in his most splendid robes and set fire to the building. With his demise in that fiery inferno, the Shang dynasty came to an end.

Review Questions

1. How did King Tang organize his kingdom?
2. Describe the Shang army.
3. What was the basic layout of Anyang?
4. What crops did the farmers grow?
5. What were the religious duties of the king?
6. Why was the dragon considered good?
7. Describe a Chinese dragon.
8. How were the oracle bones used to predict the future?
9. Why was it important for the king's astronomers to study the heavens?
10. Describe the Shang calendar.
11. How were the bronze vessels made?
12. According to legend, how was silk discovered?
13. Why did the Shang place so many valuable objects in the tombs of their rulers?
14. What sort of a person was Lady Hao?
15. What did the conjunction of the planets in the heavens mean to the ancient Chinese?
16. What caused the decline of the Shang dynasty?

Projects

1. You've learned about the friendly dragon of China. Find out about the far deadlier dragon described in the mythology of medieval Europe. Then make a chart (or a Venn Diagram), comparing and contrasting the two creatures.

To make a Venn Diagram, draw two large overlapping circles. In the part in which the circles overlap, write the similarities. In the outer part of one circle, write down attributes of the Chinese dragon that are different from the European one. In the outer part of the other circle, write down the attributes of the European dragon that are different from the Chinese one.

2. On a piece of poster board, draw a picture of a Chinese dragon face to face with its European equivalent. Or make figures of the two types of dragon out of paper or clay.

3. Pretend you are a Shang bronzesmith. Make a model of a vase out of clay. When it is dry, take a large hunk of wet clay. Cut it into four equal parts. Using a black marker, divide your model into four parts. Then press a piece of wet clay against each quarter of the model to make a set of molds. Then make a vase similar to the model but smaller. Roll a chunk of clay into a flat square slightly larger than the large vase. Place the smaller model in the middle of the clay square. Then connect the four molds around the smaller model. There should be a small space between the small model and the molds. Let everything dry. Then heat up a batch of wax and pour it into the space between the molds and the clay core. Let it harden. Then carefully break the mold with a hammer and remove the pieces. You now have a wax copy of the original clay vase. If you had used bronze, you would have a bronze vase. The wax is too delicate to allow you to break up the inner clay core, but if your copy had been made of bronze, this would be the next step.

4. Some historians have compared the Shang nobles to the Greek kings described in the poems of Homer. Like the Shang, the Greeks lived in fortress-like castles and swept across battlefields in horse-drawn chariots. Do some research on the warriors described in Homer's famous epic, *The Iliad*. See if you can find other ways in which the Shang resembled the Greek warriors. Make a chart or a poster to demonstrate the similarities and differences.

5. The Shang predicted the future by studying the cracks in "oracle bones." The ancient Greeks sought the answers to their questions about the future at special temples known as oracles. The most famous is the Oracle of Delphi. Find out more about the Greek oracles and write a short report.

6. The tomb of King Tutankamen of Egypt was the only burial site we know about in ancient Egypt that was not robbed (apart from a small theft) until it was excavated in the early 20th century. Find out more about King Tut's tomb. What similarities do you see between it and the tomb of Lady Hao? Make a poster about these two ancient tombs. Summarize the main data you've learned about them, and illustrate them with drawings, xeroxed pictures, or graphics downloaded from the Internet.

7. Write an upbeat advertisement about the Shang Dynasty, urging modern tourists to enter a time machine and visit this fascinating civilization.

8. Write several paragraphs to summarize what you've learned about the Shang dynasty.

Happenings Elsewhere in the Ancient World During the Shang Dynasty

Mycenean Civilization develops in Greece (1600 BC)

Minoan palaces destroyed in Crete (1450 BC)

Phonetic alphabet in Phoenicia (c 1400 BC)

Height of Egyptian empire (c 1300 BC)

Hitite Empire at peak in Middle East (1300 BC)

Olmec civilization in Mexico (c 1200 BC)

Exodus of Jews from Egypt (c 1240 BC)

Trojan War, Greece vs. Troy (c 1200 BC)

THE CHINESE ZODIAC

According to the ancient storytellers, the Yellow Emperor decided one day that the people on earth needed some kind of guide to help them through their many activities and undertakings. So he decided to create the zodiac. The zodiac is a circular diagram of the heavens, divided into twelve constellations and symbols. Each symbol represents certain human qualities and fates. To help him decide upon the symbols, the Emperor announced to all the animals that there would be a race, and the first twelve to cross the finish line would be chosen to stand forever as signs of human character and destiny.

On the eve of the great race all the animals went to sleep early, in order to be fresh for the start at dawn. During the night Ox suddenly awoke and thought: "I am so slow that if I am to have a chance of being selected I had better start now." So he did, but as he passed by the other sleeping animals he woke Rat. This sly rodent guessed his plan and thought: "I am so small that no matter how hard I run, even Ox will beat me." So he scurried up a tree and dropped so lightly on to Ox's back as he passed below that the great beast did not notice.

At dawn the other animals awoke and discovered that Ox and Rat had gone. They raced off after them as fast as they could, but no matter how fast they ran they could not catch up. When the finish line came into view, they saw Ox comfortably ahead of them and about to cross the line. Then Ox paused to look back to see if anyone was close. But as he paused, Rat leaped off his back and raced across the line.

This is why Rat comes first in the zodiac, followed by Ox and then all the rest of the twelve animals (Tiger, Hare, Dragon, Snake, Horse, Sheep, Monkey, Rooster, Dog, and Pig). And the reason cats chase rats is that Rat had promised to awaken Cat for the race (and didn't!); she (Cat) missed her place in the zodiac by oversleeping.

Every year in the Chinese calendar is associated with one of the twelve animals. The Year of the Rat is followed by that of the Ox and so on until the Year of the Pig, after which the cycle begins again. The Dragon is the only creature in the zodiac credited with supernatural powers, so it is particularly lucky to be born in the Year of the Dragon. Look at the zodiac chart in the Appendix at the end of this book. Read the list of character traits for people born in "your" year. Do any of them apply to you?

CHAPTER 3

THE ZHOU DYNASTY
(1022 — 222 BC)
BOOKS, BATTLES, AND BELLS

Once he defeated the Shang army, Wu founded the Zhou (Joe) dynasty. The new dynasty would last nearly 800 years, longer than any other in Chinese history. Although the later centuries of their rule were marked by incessant civil wars, the Zhou gave China some of its most enduring traditions.

Historians divide the Zhou period into two major parts — the Western Zhou and the Eastern Zhou. The names refer to the location of the capital during each time period.

The Western Zhou
(1022 – 771 BC)

A New Capital

King Wu built his capital near Chang-an (modern *Xian*, SHEE ahn) on the banks of the Wei River. The Wei flows into the Yellow River at the place where it (the Yellow River) completes its great loop and turns eastward toward the sea.

The city was a perfect square, measuring three miles on a side. (Just like Anyang!) Within the walls were nine lengthwise roads and nine others crossing these at right angles. Each avenue was nine chariot tracks wide. (Here's yet another example of the importance of the number nine in Chinese culture.)

The Duke of Zhou

In ancient times, it was expected that a conquering warrior would eliminate (murder) all surviving members of the ruling family he had defeated. King Wu, however, took a more lenient approach, and he has been praised for his humane qualities

Highlights of This Chapter

The Duke of Zhou
Feudalism in China
The Mandate of Heaven
The First Books
The Spring and Autumn Period
The Warring States
The Art of War
The Odes of Chu
Lacquerware

ever since. He spared the Shang royal family, and he even allowed a son of Di Xin to rule the little state of Song, so that he could continue to offer sacrifices to his ancestors.

Wu died only six years after his victory over the Shang. Because his son and heir (Cheng) was only an infant, the dead king's brother, the Duke of Zhou, was appointed regent. (A regent is someone who governs a kingdom when the legitimate ruler is too young to do so.) According to legend, when Wu first fell ill the Duke had appealed — in vain — to his ancestral spirits to take his own life rather than that of his brother. This is one of the many reasons why he was beloved by his people.

The Duke was an able ruler. He expanded the kingdom until he firmly controlled the entire plain of the Yellow River. Following the example of King Tang the Victorious (the first Shang king), he gave large tracts of land to some of his relatives and trusted allies. He placed members of the Shang royal family in charge of regions in the eastern part of the kingdom. He built an eastern city, Luoyang, and sent officials there to live and to keep him informed of the local happenings.

The Duke continued the traditions of the Shang. He also established elaborate new court rituals to add dignity and pomp to the Zhou government. Even the most ordinary function was often accompanied by the beating of gongs and chimes, a musical performance, and the burning of incense.

The Feudal System

The Duke of Zhou created an intricate system of mutual obligations between the king and his noblemen. It even extended to the rest of the population. The system was based upon the concept that all the land belonged to the king and that all the people were subject to his will. Historians often compare it to the feudal system that sprang up in medieval Europe 1500 years later. Here's how it worked.

The men who ruled the large territories of the kingdom (they were known as lords) ran their own local governments and collected taxes in the form of grain and

A good example of the court rituals favored by the Zhou was the elaborate ceremony that formalized the granting of a new piece of land. The most important part of the ceremony was the awarding of presents from the king to the new lord. At first, these were small and symbolic gifts, such as a piece of earth representing the soil of the newly acquired land. Over the years, the gifts became more lavish. We know about these because it was customary to commemorate the ceremony as well as the gifts with inscriptions on bronze vessels.

other produce from the people who lived there. The farmland was divided into sections of nine squares, with eight families farming one square each for themselves and the center square together. (Crops harvested from this square belonged to the lord.)

Each lord had his own army of charioteers (known as knights) and foot soldiers. The knights served as government officials when they weren't engaged in warfare. (In this regard, the Chinese knights were very different from the knights of medieval Europe, who were illiterate warriors focused solely upon combat.)

The lords owed certain duties to the king in exchange for the land he had given them. Most important, they had to appear at court in the capital city whenever summoned and to provide the king with military support when he needed it. They also supplied peasants from their territory to work on "public projects," like the construction of roads, royal palaces, and tombs. The king, for his part, was obliged to protect his subjects from any invaders who threatened his borders.

As the Zhou kings acquired more land, they passed pieces of it on to new allies. They joined the ranks of the lords. The network of duties and obligations expanded to accomodate them. This system functioned smoothly for quite a while. It provided a structure for Zhou society, with distinct social classes — the king was at the top, of course, followed by the knights/officials, craftsmen, and farmers (peasants). The system also ensured that there were armed strongholds at strategic points throughout the kingdom for added defense.

The Zhou Armies

But despite the neat system the Duke of Zhou had put into place, the kingdom was not always peaceful. As in Shang times, local leaders (the lords) frequently fought among themselves over pieces of land, and, of course, there were occasional attacks from invading tribesmen to be dealt with by the kings army.

On the battlefield, the knights wore suits of armor fashioned from small rectangular pieces of leather that were joined together with hemp fibers or silken thread. This armor was fairly flexible, allowing considerable freedom of movement. The lords wore breastplates — large pieces of hardened leather — on which were painted bright designs representing their domains. The same designs appeared on the flags their armies carried into battle. The lords and knights rode in chariots that were lighter and more elegant than those of the Shang. They carried bronze-tipped spears. The bulk of the army was made up of foot soldiers recruited from the peasants. They were armed with spears and halberds — and sometimes farm tools, like pitchforks!

The lords followed a strict code of

conduct, much like the code of chivalry of medieval Europe. No one could kill a defeated enemy or attack an opponent before he had time to mobilize his forces. Any leader who didn't "play by the rules" was shunned in Zhou society.

The Mandate of Heaven

The Shang kings, as you know, were also high priests, who served as intermediaries between the spirits and the people. The Zhou kings went a step further, tracing their descent directly from a supreme deity known as Heaven (*Tian*). (*Tian* replaced *Shang Di* as "super spirit.") Each king who came to the throne was considered a Son of Heaven, who had been given wisdom and power by his divine ancestor. This gift of authority was known as the Mandate of Heaven.

As the Son of Heaven, a king was expected to be wise, hardworking, unselfish, and successful on the battlefield. And, of course, he had to perform special rituals to honor all spirits and to appeal to them on behalf of his people.

But if a king neglected his sacred duties and acted selfishly, the spirits would display their displeasure through such natural disasters as floods, earthquakes, or famines. If he failed to heed such warnings, Heaven would withdraw its Mandate. The people would then rebel against the king and overthrow him. Heaven would eventually bestow its divine Mandate upon someone else who proved himself worthy of the honor.

This sort of thinking encouraged integrity and high moral standards among the Zhou rulers. It also provided a means for a new dynasty to justify seizing the throne from an "unworthy" man.

The Mandate of Heaven was first officially mentioned in a speech given by the Duke of Zhou. He had just defeated a rebellion led by the survivors of the Shang dynasty. (Yes, despite his lenient treatment of the defeated Shang, some of them *did* try to seize back power.) In the speech, the Duke ordered the rebels to submit to the will of Heaven, which had reclaimed power from the immoral Shang and bestowed it upon the Zhou. (This famous speech was preserved orally for hundreds of years before it was finally written down.) When King Wu's son, Chang, later came of age, the Duke quietly stepped aside and let the young king accept the Mandate of Heaven.

Beginning with the reign of King Mu (947 BC), the more significant orders (usually those related to military events) were preserved by inscribing them on bronze vessels. These inscriptions, like those made during the transfer of land ownership, are a useful source of information about the workings of the Zhou government.

The First Books

The working day of a Zhou king began at dawn, when he met with his officials in a special room in his palace. His orders for the day were written on strips of bamboo and read aloud at the meeting by the court historian. Then the strips were distributed to the appropriate officials.

The strips were actually slices of the inner pith of the bamboo plant that had been dried in the sun. They were about a foot long and 1/4 inch thick. The strips provided an excellent writing surface and were ideal for keeping government records.

As you know, Chinese writing consisted of characters that evolved from pictographs (picture writing). In Zhou times, a scribe wrote his characters from the top of a bamboo strip to the bottom, if necessary continuing the message at the top of another strip. He wrote with a bamboo brush tipped with tufts of animal hair, which he dipped in ink made of soot mixed with water.

When not in use, the bamboo strips were stacked up and tied together with silken cords. These were China's first books. (The modern character for book is a picture of a bundle of long, narrow strips held together by a thin cord.) When the records needed to be consulted, the cords were untied and the strips were lined up. They were read from right to left, beginning with the characters at the top of the first strip on the right. This helps explain why modern Chinese is often written in columns, starting in the upper right-hand corner. (A traditional Chinese book begins at what English readers would consider the last page.)

The Zhou also wrote books on particular subjects. In fact, some of the most important volumes in Chinese history were written during the Western Zhou period. These include *The Book of Documents*, *The Book of Songs*, and *The Book of Changes*. Let's take a closer look.

The Book of Documents

The Book of Documents (*Shujing*) is China's oldest history text and our chief source of information about the earliest period of Chinese history. It contains the legends about the first Chinese rulers, mythical and real. Some of these tales had been passed on orally for centuries before they were written down. Others were composed in Zhou times and reflect what people living then thought such legendary figures as the Three Sages (remember them?) *might* have said and done.

The Book of Documents includes speeches given by kings and other political

From the time of the first appearance of *The Book of Documents*, Chinese historians would traditionally group the Shang and the Zhou together with the Xia as the Three Ancient Dynasties.

figures at important historical moments. Among these are the Duke of Zhou's speech about the Mandate of Heaven. The book describes the Zhou conquest of the Shang as the victory of just and noble warriors over decadent courtiers led by a dissolute king who had lost the Mandate of Heaven. Because of these accounts, the final rulers of the Xia and Shang (Jie and Di Xin) would long be remembered as examples of evil and unworthy kings.

The Book of Documents puts King Wen, King Wu, and the Duke of Zhou in the "big picture" of Chinese history by linking them with the super heroes of China's mythical past. Like those mythical rulers, they modeled the qualities required for the establishment and leadership of an enduring government.

One chapter in *The Book of Documents* is considered China's earliest text on geography. It divides the country into nine regions (yes, nine!), according to the natural features of the landscape. The locations of the nine regions would seem inaccurate if you were to look at the map. This is because ancient Chinese maps were always drawn with the south on top and the north on the bottom. (Why? The south, which was associated with heat and the bright sun, was the most important direction. So, of course, it had to go on the top.)

The Book of Songs

The Book of Songs (*Shijing*) is the earliest collection of Chinese poetry. It was compiled in the 7th century BC from poems probably dating back several hundred years earlier.

Ancient Chinese poetry was sung rather than spoken, often to the accompaniment of a flute or stringed instrument. Many of the 305 poems included in *The Book of Songs* were sung at court during important ceremonies. Some celebrate the exploits of the early Zhou rulers. Others are more solemn and probably accompanied ritual sacrifices of food to the spirits of the royal ancestors. There are also odes of praise, ballads exalting China's mythical founders and culture heroes, lyrics about the pleasant lifestyle of the nobles, and charming, often humorous love songs. (One verse exclaims, "Disorder does not come

Music has always played an important role in Chinese society. The history of musical instruments goes back to Neolithic times. As early as 6000 BC, people were playing seven-hole flutes in the Yellow River valley for pure entertainment. *The Book of Songs* lists 29 different types of percussion, wind, and stringed instruments. These include bamboo and bone flutes, bronze bells, stone chimes, drums (covered with animal skins), zithers and lutes (with silk strings and wooden bodies). Actually, the character for music is also translated as "pleasure."

down from Heaven – it is produced by women!")

Some of the poems probably originated as folk songs. They expressed the sorrows and pleasures of everyday life in the countryside, with wonderful descriptions of ordinary people at work clearing fields, planting seeds, harvesting crops, gathering mulberry leaves for silkworms, and even complaining about tax collectors.

The Book of Changes

Remember the Shang oracle bones? By Zhou times, that method of predicting the future had been largely abandoned. Now the priests looked for answers in a divination manual called *The Book of Changes (Yijing)*. The ideas expressed in the manual are based upon the belief that human destiny is related to the ever-changing relationship between the two great forces of nature, the *yin* and *yang*.

Remember how Pangu separated the two forces, with everything *yin* — being cool and dark — sinking to the earth, while everything *yang* — being warm and bright — rose to the heavens? Over the centuries, the concept of *yin* was extended to include everything that was passive, negative, restful, or female. It also applied to the earth itself, as well as water and the moon. *Yang* now included everything that was active, strong, positive, or masculine, and also fire, heaven, and the sun.

The two forces were not opposites. Rather, they were dual aspects of nature that were in constant fluctuation, one giving way as the other expands. For example, day (*yang*) gave way to night (*yin*), summer (*yang*) to winter (*yin*), and back again, the cycle continuing forever. The *yin* and *yang* were symbolized by a circle, divided between the dark *yin* and the light *yang*. Within each was a part of the other, showing that the two forces were intimately bound to one another.

In *The Book of Changes* arrangements of broken and unbroken lines which represent *yin* and *yang* are interpreted to predict the future. The broken lines stand for *yin*, while the unbroken lines stand for *yang*. The lines are arranged in groups of three, one atop the other. These groups are called trigrams. There are eight possible combinations of broken and unbroken lines (and therefore eight possible trigrams).

The trigrams were originally made with the stems of the yarrow plant. When a question was asked, the diviner randomly selected long and short stems and placed them in a series of trigrams. Each of the trigrams represented an element of nature. For example, a solid line on top, broken line in the middle, and solid line on bottom represented fire, while a trigram with the solid line in the middle and broken lines on top and bottom meant water.

And there was more. Two trigrams formed a hexagram. There were 64 possible combinations of broken and unbroken lines in a hexagram (or 64 possible hexagrams). If a questioner's choice resulted in the hexagram meaning "water over fire," this was interpreted as "conquest" or "success," since water conquers fire by quenching its flames.

The ancient diviners claimed that legendary emperor Fuxi (one of the Three Sovereigns) had created the eight basic trigrams after observing the patterns in a tortoise shell. These trigrams and their meanings were supposedly passed down orally until about 1142 BC, when King Wen is said to have arranged them into 64 hexagrams and then recorded these groupings and their meanings on strips of bamboo.

In later centuries, a single trigram came to represent many things — a person-

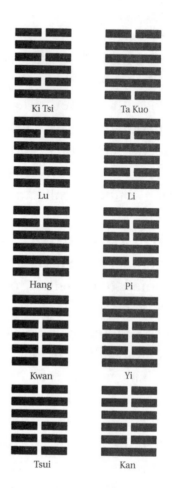

Ki Tsi   Ta Kuo

Lu   Li

Hang   Pi

Kwan   Yi

Tsui   Kan

The meanings of the above hexagrams are as follows: Ki Tsi (serious setbacks); Ta Kuo (a dangerous position); Lu (travel or homelessness); Li (need for correct behavior); Hang (a happy marriage); Pi (deceptive appearances); Kwan (the need for objectivity); Yi (success and travel); Tsui (a political encounter); and Kan (a military retreat).

al characteristic, a body part, a time, a number, an element of the universe, a planet, a color, a direction, and an animal. As you can see, fortune-telling became very complicated! You'll learn more about these symbols in Chapter 5.

Busy Craftsmen

The Western Zhou thrived for over two centuries. The government ran efficiently, the farmers had abundant harvests, and most people were content.

Craftsmen were kept busy. Bronze smiths produced great numbers of handsomely decorated vessels as well as weapons and tools. The first metal coins were made around 750 BC. These replaced the cowrie shells that had been used as mediums of exchange. The coins were shaped liked knives, hoes, and spades, the most useful implements in that farming society.

Around 600 BC Zhou craftsmen learned to create high enough temperatures to smelt iron ore. They were, in fact, the very first to make cast iron by adding carbon to the molten metal. (The West did not learn to cast iron for another thousand years.) Iron is a much tougher metal than bronze.

Down On The Farm

The use of iron-tipped plows made it possible for farmers to bring new lands under cultivation and to produce more grain than ever before. People living in hilly areas increased the size of their fields by building terraces in the loess soil.

The use of fertilizers made it possible to grow crops in the same fields year after year instead of having to abandon worn-out fields for new ones. The source of the fertilizers might surprise you. There were not many farm animals in China. Having an ox to pull a plow was something of a luxury for a peasant, since these big beasts consumed a great deal of feed. Because there was a limited supply of manure, human excrement was collected and deposited on the fields. (It was called "night soil.")

The Lords Gain More Power

The feudal system worked largely because no one questioned the authority of the ruler. King Yi, who lived in the late 800's BC, flaunted his power by ordering the Duke of Ai boiled to death because the nobleman had dared to criticize him. Just a decade later, however, the situation began to change. Because the later kings were less competent that their predecessors, the lords became very independent. Sometimes they completely ignored royal commands. (Didn't the same thing happen at the end of the Shang dynasty?)

In 771 BC, King You passed over his

The first fishing reel was developed about this time from a battle device designed to retrieve a spear after it had been thrown at an enemy.

legitimate heir, Ping, in favor of the son of a concubine. This was a bold move, since the sons of the king's first wife traditionally had precedence over those of his secondary wives (his concubines). The inner circle of advisors immediately began fighting over who should inherit the throne.

As we've seen, in-fighting among the courtiers could lead to grave consequences. This was certainly the case in 770 BC, when a group of noblemen took advantage of the confusion and allied themselves with bands of nomadic tribesmen living near the western border of the kingdom. An unlikely army of charioteers, foot soldiers, and barbarian horsemen attacked and sacked the Zhou capital. In the process, King You was slain.

The Eastern Zhou
(770 — 221 BC)

A Move to Luoyang

The victors set up You's disinherited son (Ping) in Luoyang, making this eastern city the new capital. Thus began the period of the Eastern Zhou.

The young king (King Ping!) knew that his fate was in the hands of the rebel lords, so he did whatever they told him to do. He was what you'd call a puppet king. From this time on, the Zhou kings had no effective political or military power beyond a small area surrounding Luoyang. Although the dynasty continued for another 500 years, the kings' only major function was to conduct religious rituals in the name of the Chinese people. The lords, meanwhile, became rulers of their own mini-kingdoms.

The centuries that followed the fall of the Western Zhou were tumultuous ones. To add some sort of order, historians have further divided the era of the Eastern Zhou into two major parts: the Spring and Autumn Period and the Period of the Warring States.

The Spring and Autumn Period

Rivals for Power

The Spring and Autumn Period gets its name from a chronicle kept by the dukes of the small kingdom of Lu — *The Annals of the Spring and Autumn*. The chronicle covers the years between 722 and 481 BC. It describes the decline of Zhou royal authori-

The Annals of the Spring and Autumn marks the beginning of the Chinese tradition of recording histories of individual states and, when the country was later unified under an emperor, of each ruling dynasty.

ty and documents the activities of a succession of strong leaders of rival kingdoms who, by force of arms, maintained a balance of power in northern China.

These were troubling times. The larger, more powerful kingdoms were tightly organized military states, constantly on the lookout for any threat of attack. The rulers of these states jockeyed for position, forming alliances when it suited their interests and then breaking them when it no longer did. It was not unusual for one man to take the title of king (*Wang*), despite the fact that the Zhou king was still very much alive and well in the city of Luoyang. It was a violent age, marked by such gruesome sights as the cut-off ears of enemies displayed at ancestral temples and the blood of captives spread upon ceremonial drums.

The best known leader of this period is Duke Huan of Qi. He went to war 28 times in 42 years. (Organizing a military campaign every other year for such a long period certainly belongs in the record books!) But the Duke also tried hard to keep the peace. In 651 BC he invited representatives of five major kingdoms to a meeting, where he got them to agree to a set of principles of good government and peaceful coexistence. Unfortunately, the alliance did not last and warfare continued to be the norm.

The Game of War

Do you remember the code of conduct set in motion in the days of the Duke of Zhou? (See page 32 if you've forgotten.) Duke Xiang of Song followed its rules to the letter. In 638 BC, he refused to launch a decisive attack against his enemies, despite the advice of his generals. He held back because the enemies had not had time to arrange themselves in perfect combat formation after crossing a river. Since he refused to take advantage of the enemy's weakness, his men suffered a heavy defeat. (In the 20th century, Mao Zedong often remarked, "Who do you take me for, the Duke of Song?," when he was questioned about taking action.)

Sometimes war seemed more like a game than serious business. A tale was told about three warriors from the kingdom of Chu. They sped past the front lines of an enemy army in their chariots, unleashing

Cold Food Day is a holiday celebrated for centuries that originated during the Spring and Autumn Period. It was intended to remind the people of Jie Zhi Tui, who served Prince Chong Er loyally during this era. When Jie died in a fire, Chong Er declared an annual festival in his memory. Kitchen fires were put out and no cooking was done. (This explains why it was called Cold Food Day.) In later centuries, children in the emperor's palace would compete to be the first to kindle a new fire by twirling sticks on wooden boards.

arrows as they galloped by. As the enemy charioteers pursued them toward their own lines, they saw the three take off after a stag that had suddenly emerged from the woods. When they caught up with them, the three had killed the stag, which they then chivalrously offered to their pursuers. The incident ended with the enemy charioteers joyfully carrying the carcass back to share with their comrads.

Bells of Bronze

Although warfare was a common occurence, the nobles always found time to enjoy music. Lord Yi of Zeng (who died in 433 BC) must have loved listening to music, since his tomb contained 124 different instruments. Among them were drums, bamboo flutes, panpipes, mouth organs, zithers, and a set of 32 chimestones. The most spectacular item in his tomb was a set of 65 perfectly preserved bronze bells. They were arranged in decreasing order of size on a three-tiered wooden frame.

The smallest bell weighs 5 pounds and is 8 inches high, while the largest is 61 inches high and weighs 449 pounds. The sides of the bells bear inscriptions indicating their tones when struck with a wooden cane or mallet. Each bell actually produces two notes, one if struck in the center and another if struck to one side.

Even today, the bells are perfectly tuned and can be played. The Chinese music scale has only five notes, as compared with Western music, which has twelve in an octave (whole notes plus sharps and flats). And Chinese music does not have harmony. Bells and chimestones such as those found in Lord Li's tomb also served as standard setters for an orchestra, providing the notes to which the other instruments were tuned.

The lord's tomb also contained a huge bell weighing 5,500 pounds! Imagine the ingenuity required simply to cast such a giant bronze. The bell produces a beautiful deep tone.

Big Fish Eat the Little Ones

By the end of the Spring and Autumn Period, the methods of warfare had begun to change. For one thing, chariots were replaced by cavalry (mounted horsemen).

Metal bells evolved from scoops that were used to measure grain. They were usually struck with a wooden stick. Over the years, bronze smiths learned to cast elaborately decorated bronze bells. In Zhou times, a set of such bells was a symbol of the status, wealth, and power of a lord. They were played on important occasions, such as banquets and religious rituals. Today, China's largest bronze bell hangs in the Great Bell Temple in Beijing. It is 18 feet high and weighs 63 tons! When struck, it can be heard 15 miles away.

The Chinese had been influenced by the awesome tactics of the nomadic tribesmen, who launched their attacks at a full gallop, riding nearly shoulder to shoulder and shooting a volley of arrows. (They guided their mounts with their legs.) The lords also began putting more effort into training their soldiers. Gradually, the old formation of nobles riding in chariots at the head of a troop of peasants gave way to mounted officers commanding massive armies of well-disciplined foot soldiers. By the middle of the 6th century, armies numbered as many as 600,000 men.

With the changes in military techniques, the more powerful states began to swallow up the smaller ones. Although there were 170 independent "mini-kingdoms" at the beginning of the Spring and Autumn Period, only about a dozen remained in 500 BC.

The Period of the Warring States

The Seven Super Powers

The Warring States Period began in 403 BC. This final era of the Zhou dynasty gets its name from a historical work compiled two centuries after it came to an end — *Intrigues of the Warring States*. During this period, seven "warring states" fought for supremacy in Inner China. These were the kingdoms of the Zhao, Wei, Han, Qin, Qi,

Yan and Chu. (Find them on the map of the Warring States on the next page.)

The Art of War

It was at this time that long iron swords and flexible scale armor (iron plates joined by metal rivets or silken ties) became readily available for the Zhou warrior. The invention of the crossbow in the 4th century BC enabled archers to shoot pointed metal bolts, released by a trigger mechanism, a long distance. (The crossbows were mass-produced by specialized workers and had interchangeable parts.)

With the improved weapons and large armies, military specialists appeared

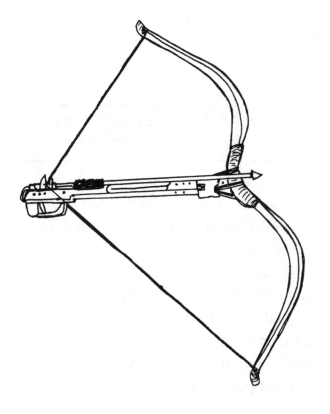

Yan

Zhao

Qi

Yellow Sea

Wei

Yellow River

Qin

Han

Chu

Yangzi River

The Warring States

on the scene. *The Art of War* was written by such a man, Sunzi, to discuss battle tactics. It was the first book of its kind. Sunzi scoffed at the earlier heroic vision of war, in which lords bravely charged across the field of battle at the head of their army of footsoldiers. He believed success in war depended upon the commander's skill in gathering information about his enemy and striking at his weakest points. He emphasized the importance of cunning and deceit — tricking an opponent into believing he intended to do one thing and then, suddenly, doing something completely different. An army should move with great speed, he counseled, and a leader should never let his own men know his strategy. That way, they would need to wait quietly and at full attention to act upon his every command.

The Art of War became the main

source of military theory throughout eastern Asia, and it later influenced generals in the West. (A French version appeared in the 18th century.)

A Thriving Economy

The centuries of fighting disrupted the settled patterns of farming in China. As land ownership became concentrated in fewer and fewer hands, the old relationships between lord and peasant disappeared. And worries about a violent death on the battlefield joined the threat of bad harvests and famine among the woes of the struggling farmers.

And yet, despite the disruptions, Chinese culture continued to thrive. Cities grew in size and number, as merchants carried trade goods between them. The growing class of merchants were despised by members of the old landed nobility. They looked down on anyone who became wealthy through his own efforts. The nobles had relied on favors from the court and the labor of their own subjects for income. They greatly resented the way the merchants were acquiring wealth, and they passed laws to keep them from taking official posts.

Working with Lacquer

A major craft of the Eastern Zhou was lacquerware. Lacquer is a natural resin produced by the lacquer tree (*Rhus verniciflua*), which grows in the basin area of the Yellow River. Lacquer hardens to form a smooth, hard, protective coating (or varnish) that looks something like plastic. The ancient Chinese found it somewhat of a wonder product for making objects waterproof and heat-resistant.

Techniques used to obtain and process the lacquer resin were developed as early as Neolithic times. The resin was tapped from a tree by making cuts in the bark, and it was collected, drop by drop, in special containers. It was then boiled for a long time to increase its density. Gradually, the resin turned into a viscous liquid with a pale amber color. Now it was ready to use.

In earliest times, lacquer was applied to carved wooden objects, such as spoons and cups, in very thin layers. (One layer had to be completely dry before the next coat was added.) This process required a temperature of between 77 and 86 degrees F with a high level of humidity (80-85 per cent). Otherwise, the lacquer would not solidify. When the final coat was dry, the surface of the object was polished with very fine clay, charcoal ash, or powdered deer horn.

The lacquer coating was totally resistant to water, corrosive acids, and heat, which explains why so many objects covered with lacquer have survived all these centuries. A well-preserved lacquered cup was found in the grave goods in a tomb dating from about 3000 BC, and remains of coated wooden coffins date from about 2000 BC. Shang craftsmen produced elaborate lacquerware that imitated the designs of bronzes made at the same period. To do this, they molded thin strips of wood into the shapes of bowls and goblets by softening and bending them with steamed heat. Then they coated them with lacquer.

It wasn't long before the craftsmen learned to apply lacquer to other surfaces, such as bronze, clay, leather, bamboo, paper, and cloth (hemp). In the 4th century BC, a new technique was invented that involved placing several layers of lacquer-saturated cloth on a clay mold. When the coating was dry, the mold was broken and removed. Now the lacquered cloth could stand on its own.

Lacquer was often colored with mineral or vegetable pigments, usually red or black. The red came from cinnebar, an ore containing mercury sulfide that has a deep vermillion color. Black was made from soot. In later centuries, Chinese craftsmen would carve objects thickly coated with lacquer into exquisite works of art.

The Odes of Chu

Around 300 BC, the second great collection of Chinese poems appeared. This is known as the *Odes of Chu*, a reference to the kingdom of Chu where the poems were written. These works are filled with rich imagery of the lush countryside of the Yangzi region. Most have religious themes — one is the song of a goddess summoning a soul to guide it in its journey to the afterlife. Compared to the earthy qualities of the verses in *The Book of Songs*, the *Odes* evoke a whimsical world of myth and magic.

The most famous of these is entitled "Encountering Sorrow." It is one of 25 poems written by Qu Yuan. (He is the first prominent poet in Chinese history.) Qu Yuan was born to an aristocratic family in the state of Qu (in the Yangzi River valley). He held a high position at the Qu court until he was slandered by men jealous of him and banished. When the king of Qu (King Huai) was later captured and his capital seized by the Qin, a despondent Qu Yuan wrote his famous poem.

According to the legend, after Qu Yuan threw himself into the river, the local people tried to find him to give him a proper funeral and burial. They launched their boats into the river and threw rice overboard, hoping the hungry fish (or evil spirits) would eat the rice instead of the body as they searched for it. This is the origin of the popular Dragon-boat Festival, which is held today in southern China on the fifth day of the fifth lunar month to commemorate the poet's spirit.

The highlight of the festival is race of long boats shaped like dragons. Spectators clang cymbals and gongs and wave colorful flags to cheer on their favorite. Later, everyone eats sweet rice dumplings, reminders of the searchers' desperate hunt for the poet and the rice they tossed to the fish.

Many critics consider "Encountering Sorrow" the finest Chinese poem ever written. It describes the poet's travels and experiences, his fall from favor in the Qu court, and even an imaginary visit to Heaven. (Heaven — *Tian* — was sometimes viewed as an all-powerful deity, sometimes as the place where all the spirits lived.) Soon after writing the poem, Qu Yuan committed suicide by drowning in the Miluyo River (in Hunan province). He was remembered as the model of an unappreciated yet loyal minister.

A New Class of Thinkers

The last Zhou king was killed by the Qin in 256. This ended the Zhou dynasty, but the Warring States Period continued a bit longer. You'll see how all the fighting finally came to an end in Chapter 5. But before moving on, it's important to learn about some exciting intellectual developments that were taking place.

Do you remember the knights, who served as officials (as well as warriors) in the feudal states of the Western Zhou? To aid the knights in their official work, the lords arranged to have certain talented commoners (peasants) trained in special schools. From this group, known as the *shi*, would arise an entire class of scribes, chroniclers, and philosophers.

Beginning in the Spring and Autumn Period, certain members of the *shi* roved about China, offering their counsel to any ruler who would listen to them. The most enlightened ruler of the time, King Huan of Qi (remember him?), welcomed numerous scholars to his court.

Certain of the *shi* proposed ideas that would profoundly affect the development of Chinese culture. For this reason, the era of the Eastern Zhou is considered the Golden Age of Chinese philosophy. You'll learn about these ideas in the next chapter.

REVIEW QUESTIONS

1. How did King Wu deal with the survivors of the Shang dynasty?

2. What obligations did the lords have to the king?

3. What were the advantages of having a feudal system?

4. What was the Mandate of Heaven?

5. What materials were used to make the first books?

6. How did *The Book of Documents* add prestige to the Zhou rulers?

7. Describe briefly *The Book of Songs*.

8. Explain the concept of *yin* and *yang*.

9. How were the trigrams used to predict the future?

10. What caused the fall of the Western Zhou?

11. What were the two main periods of the Eastern Zhou?

12. How were battles usually fought during the Spring and Autumn Period?

13. What were the main ideas of *The Art of War*?

14. How was lacquer obtained?

15. What is "Encountering Sorrow?"

16. Who were the *shi*?

PROJECTS

1. Consulting your library and/or the Internet, find out more about ancient Chinese music and instruments. Make a poster and share it with your classmates.

2. Ancient Chinese bronze bells had no clappers. They were struck to produce a sound. You can create the same effect with glasses of water. Take five glasses of equal size. Fill the first with an inch of water, the second about an inch and a half, the third with two inches, the fourth with two and a half inches, and the fifth with three inches. Then take a fork and strike each glass. Notice how each produces a different sound. Experiment a bit, and then see if you can play a simple tune.

3. Sunzi has often been compared to Machiavelli, a political thinker of the Italian Renaissance. Find out more about both of these men. Then make a chart or Venn Diagram comparing them.

4. Learn more about the history of the crossbow in the eastern and western worlds. Write a short report about your findings. Be sure to include illustrations.

5. Find a copy of *The Odes of Chu*. Select several poems and read them to your classmates.

7. Consult the art books in your library for information and illustrations of lacquerware. Share them with your classmates.

8. Make a detailed timeline of the entire Zhou dynasty.

Happenings Elsewhere in the Ancient World During the Zhou Dynasty

Solomon, King of Israel (960 BC)
First Olympic Games in Greece (776 BC)
Cyrus the Great of Persia conquers Lydia and the Greek cities in Anatolia (545 BC)
Birth of Buddha in India (533 BC)
Founding of Rome (753 BC)
Greek Golden Age (461-431 BC)
Socrates (469-399 BC)
Alexander the Great conquers Persia (334-328) BC

CHAPTER 4
THE PHILOSOPHERS
HOW TO BE HAPPY

The disorder and turmoil of the Eastern Zhou Period must have made many thoughtful people long for the "good old days" when the Duke of Zhou ruled China. What had happened to the Mandate of Heaven? Where was the leader who could restore order? Would families ever be able to contemplate the beauty of the sunrise without worrying about enemy troops appearing on the horizon?

Scholarly men, drawn from the ranks of the *shi*, came up with all sorts of solutions for restoring order — so many, in fact, that historians would later refer to the "Hundred Schools" of political philosophy. (Political philosophy is the study of rules or principles of government.) Actually, there were not *that* many viewpoints, but there certainly was a wide range of opinions about how to solve China's current problems.

During the 6th century BC, two men proposed some solutions that would shape Chinese intellectual history for the next two thousand years. These great philosophers are known to us as Laozi (low dzoo) and Confucius (kun Fyoo shus).

Laozi Writes a Book

Laozi (his name means "Old Master") lived between 604 BC and 517 BC. Many historians believe he started out as a librarian in the household of a Zhou prince. He soon became so bothered by the petty intrigues of court life that he left his position and set off for the western mountains mounted on an ox. When a guard at the Chinese frontier asked to see his teachings, he allegedly showed him a short book he had written entitled *The Way and its Power* (*Dao De Jing*, dow duh jing). (It had only 5,000 words.) It was a collection of sayings and short poems expressing his views about life. This would become one of the most important books in China.

Highlights of This Chapter

Laozi and "The Way"
Daoism
Zhuangzi
Confucius Begins Teaching
Family Relationships
The Five Classics
The Analects
Mencius and Xunzi

Daoism

The Chinese word *dao* (dow) means "way" or "path," and Laozi used it to mean the way of nature. He contrasted the disorder of Chinese society during his time with the apparent order of the natural world. He believed the key to restoring peace lay in teaching people to be responsive to the patterns and rhythms of nature. Laozi reasoned that since humans were only small parts of a vast universe, it was foolish to try to interrupt or change the natural flow of life. Efforts to do so only upset the balance and created disorder and unhappiness.

People should accept things as they were. It was part of nature's plan that certain flowers should live for only a day, while some trees endured for centuries. Big fish ate little ones, and a single flash of lightning could destroy an entire forest. No one could change nature's plan, so why try? To use a modern term, it was best to simply "go with the flow," knowing that in time things would work themselves out, one way or another. The goal of life, said Laozi, was to blend in with the natural flow like a drop of water in the vast ocean of the universe. This approach to living came to known as *Daoism*.

For Laozi and his followers, social interaction (spending time with other people) led to greed and rivalry. They prefered to lead lives of solitude so that they could contemplate the natural world. Their only desire was to become "formless, desireless, without striving…content."

But what about the government? According to Laozi, the ideal ruler did very little. Rather than interfere with the lives of his subjects, he simply set an example of humility and acceptance of things as they were. So the best government was that which governed least. And here's the paradox: by engaging in no action, order would prevail.

Daoism appealed to many educated

Laozi's sayings reflect his taste for paradox. Here are some choice examples.

— The wise man keeps to the deed that consists in taking no action.
— The man who withdraws from the world finds it; by giving up power, he becomes powerful; by not desiring riches, he becomes rich.
— Those who strive for nothing cannot be disappointed.
— Gently flowing water can wear down the hardest rock.

And here's a saying that seems to capture the esssence of his beliefs.

— A tree does not want things; it does not struggle to control others; it just grows!

Chinese and made them feel less anxious about the political unrest of their times. In fact, many of the *shi* lost all interest in government and withdrew from public affairs, turning their attention to the world of nature. Some abandoned civilization altogether and lived as hermits in the forests or mountains.

Zhuangzi Talks to Animals

Zhuangzi (choo ang zuh) was a Daoist philosopher who lived about two centuries after Laozi. He wrote the second great book of Daoism, known as *The Zhuangzi*. It is filled with parables and fanciful episodes in which animals and insects debate philosophy and men float about in the air. At one point, the author takes the form of a butterfly and argues with fish and other creatures about the best ways to achieve happiness!

In one conversation, a man complains to the philosopher that a large tree is useless because its branches and trunk are crooked and cannot be used for lumber. Zhuangzi replies that the tree *does* have a use, since its great branches offer shade in the hot weather. The tree is only useless if you try to make it something other than what nature intended it to be. He adds that the same applies to people. Everyone should know his inner nature and adopt a lifestyle appropriate to his strengths and weaknesses. Trying to be something or someone other than you are only leads to unhappiness.

In another episode, Zhuangzi describes how he was once offered a position at court by two representatives of the Prince of Chu. After the offer was made, he gazed off toward the nearby muddy river bank for a moment, then remarked that he had heard that the Prince had a dried out sacred tortoise, two thousand years old, which he kept in a box wrapped in silk and brocade. When the officials said that this was true, Zuangzi asked them if, had it been given a choice, the tortoise would have preferred to have been alive in the mud or dead in the palace. The officials answered that, of course, it would have preferred to have been alive in the mud. Zuangzi then responded, "I, too, prefer the mud. Goodbye."

*   *   *   *   *   *   *

Despite its pleas for simplicity and acceptance of the world as it is, many people questioned the practicality of Daoism. It wasn't always possible to retreat from society, they observed, and they doubted that the social order could be restored if no one did anything about it.

Confucius

The philosopher known to Westerners as Confucius lived from 551 to 478 BC. He proposed some more practical solutions to the social and political problems of his time. (He lived during the lems of his time. (He lived during the Warring States Period.)

His actual name was Kong Qiu (kong CHEE oo) — Kong being the family name. (In Chinese, the family name is always given first.) Confucius is the latinized version of *Kong Fuzi* (Kong FOO Zuh), "Grand Master Kong," as he came to be known.

Kong Qiu was born in Qufu, a village in the small kingdom of Lu. It is said that before he was born his mother dreamed of a unicorn. This was a sign that her baby would grow up to be a great man. His father, governor of the town of Zou, was quite elderly. In fact, he was nearly 70 when he married Qiu's mother, his second wife. (She was only 15!) He died when his son was three, leaving the family without resources. Nonetheless, the boy had a good education at a local school.

Kong's first jobs were quite humble ones — keeping books for a state-owned granary and then overseeing the local grazing pastures of sheep and cattle — but he impressed his employers with his integrity and hard work. He married when he was 19 and had a son, Bo Yo. (Not much is known about his wife or son.)

When his mother died a few years later, he gave up his job and began the customary three-year mourning period, leaving the bottom of his robe unhemmed as a token of his grief. It was during this time that he devoted himself full-time to scholarship. He spent hours each day pondering the writings in *The Book of Documents,* and wondering how he could apply some of the

The Chinese unicorn (the *qilin*) was a peaceable mythical beast. Its name itself combined the characters for male and female, making the animal a living embodiment of the joining of yin and yang. The *qilin* had the body of a deer, the hooves of a horse, the tail of an ox, and, of course, a horn on its forehead. Dreaming of a unicorn was always a good omen.

became a master of the "Six Arts" required of a well-educated gentleman of that day — music, calligraphy (beautiful writing), mathematics, archery, charioteering, and the performance of ritual ceremonies.

Once the mourning period was over, Kong began a teaching career. Students wishing to become officials paid him to instruct them about history and the functions of government, and before long he had a small following of young men. Unlike many teachers, he accepted commoners as students as well as members of the aristocracy. Kong taught by asking thought-provoking questions and waiting for his students to puzzle out the answers. He praised his students for their efforts and avoided punishing or embarrassing them (as most teachers of the time were likely to do). He hoped that his students would become thoughtful advisers to government leaders.

Family Matters

Kong became convinced that social order could be restored in China if the people were provided with a set of rules to follow. People were basically good, he claimed, and they wanted to be virtuous, if they only knew how. He looked to the family as the basic unit in society, and he set up a series of strict guidelines of behavior that were intended to help each family member know his or her place and act responsibly.

For Kong Qiu, respect for one's parents was one of the highest virtues. A child should honor and obey his parents, and when they become aged, he should take care of them. This concept of the obligation of child to parent is known as *filial piety*. In Chinese writing, the character for filial piety is a symbol of a son supporting his aged father as he walks.

This view fit in well with traditional beliefs. Since the earliest dynasties, the Chinese family was headed by the eldest male of the senior generation. The family unit included cousins, uncles, and aunts as well as children and grandchildren. Several generations of relatives often lived together in one large house, each "nuclear" family having a set of rooms, like an apartment. The eldest man was absolute master of the household, just as the ruler was (in theory) the undisputed leader of Chinese society.

Beginning in Zhou times, everyone in the family was expected to kneel in front of

Peasant families could usually afford only three children. To have more sons meant dividing family land into smaller parcels for inheritance, and more girls would mean more expenses to provide dowries. If more children were born to a family than could be cared for, they were placed with relatives, abandoned, sold as laborers or even drowned at birth. Poor families often sold their daughters to be servants of the rich.

the eldest man and to touch his or her head to the floor several times (this is called a kowtow), then rise and back out of the room. When the patriarch (male leader) of the family died, he was succeeded by his eldest surviving son, and so on down through the generations.

Kong's set of guidelines also applied to the relationships between husband and wife (he was expected to respect and cherish her, she to obey and honor him) and between older and younger siblings (younger siblings were subservient to older ones).

Honoring The Dead

The death of a relative elevated the deceased person to the status of honored ancestor. Just as the ruler performed rituals to honor his divine ancestors, a grown child was expected to carry on ceremonies in respect of his or her own dead parents and other relatives.

Every home had an altar where incense was burned early each morning and at night. The smoke carried the thoughts of the family upward into the realm of the spirits. This was accompanied by reverential bowing before a portrait of an ancestor or a tablet bearing his name. On special days, each family member, in order from the most important man to the youngest child, kowtowed to the portrait or tablet. Then an offering of food would be made to the spirit of the ancestor. The food was consumed by the family following the ceremony.

In return for these rituals, the ancestral spirits were expected to protect and look after the family members. (If the spirits were not appeased in this way, they might become "hungry ghosts," scavenging in graveyards and creating misfortune for the living.)

What Is Good Government?

Kong was certain that if everyone knew his or her place in the family and understood what was expected of him and others, there would be peace and order in the community. On a larger scale, he viewed all the Chinese as a big family, with the ruler at its head.

He turned to China's mythical past for examples of good leaders. His heroes were the Three Sages — Yao, Shun, and Yu the Great. The highest praise he could find for any subsequent ruler of China was to say, "Even Yao or Shun (or Yu) could not have found cause to criticize him."

Confucius was vague about his religious beliefs. When asked about his views of the afterlife, he replied, "We do not even understand life, so how can we understand death?" His concern was with the "here and now," not the distant realm of the spirits.

found cause to criticize him."

Looking to more recent times, Kong greatly admired the virtuous leadership of the three early Zhou rulers — King Wen, King Wu, and the Duke of Zhou. Using them as models, he proposed that a ruler should strive to become a *junzi* ("perfect gentleman"), who embodied the "five virtues." The five virtues were *li* (proper conduct), *ren* (compassion and respect for all others and for nature), *xin* (trustworthiness), *yi* (righteousness and honesty), and *zhi* (understanding of himself and knowledge about right and wrong). And he must be humble, seeking "to possess ability, and yet ask of those who do not; to know much, and yet inquire of those who know little; to possess, and yet appear not to possess; to be full, and yet appear empty." If a ruler modeled these virtues, his subjects would surely follow his example, and everyone would live in harmony. Kong remarked that a leader was like the wind and the people were like the grass: when the wind blows, the grass always bends.

The Traveling Philosopher

Kong Qiu traveled to many states in the hope of persuading their leaders to follow his guidelines. He never claimed to be a sage or innovator. Rather, he considered himself a transmitter of the wisdom of earlier times.

However, the lords and princes he visited found his ideas impractical in their highly competitive and cutthroat world. They had little time to think about cultivating the five virtues when they were struggling to stay one step ahead of their enemies. So after 13 years, Kong returned to Lu and devoted himself full-time to teaching. His title of Great Master Kong (Confucius) dates from this period, so we'll now refer to him in that way.

The Five Classics

Confucius used five basic texts to teach his students. These have come to be known as the Five Classics. Four of these were books you've already learned about: *The Book of Documents*, *The Book of Changes*, *The Book of Songs*, and *The Spring* and Autumn Annals. The fifth book, *The Book of Rites*, was a collection of works on gentlemanly conduct and religious rituals.

Confucius interpreted the contents of these texts as lessons for good living and moral government. *The Book of Documents* provided examples of the humane and well-run government of the early Zhou dynasty. The patterns and predictions in *The Book of Changes* related to his principles of a well organized society. *The Book of Songs* offered a guide to understanding of the human heart, while *The Spring and Autumn Annals* contained judgments of benevolent leadership. *The Book of Rites* was a guide to proper expression of honor and respect. (He reasoned that elaborate rituals created a sense of community among the people and strenghened their sense of reverence for their superiors.)

*   *   *   *   *

Confucius believed that nobility should be based upon personal merit, not an accident of birth. This being true, shouldn't the highest government offices be open to those best qualified? Confucius certainly thought so, and he spoke about a system of examinations to select the men most capable to serve in the government. But few government leaders supported such an idea, since they were mostly the sons of noblemen who got their jobs through family connections. They had no interest in compromising the advantages of their social class. Confucius was simply ahead of his time. As you will see, within a few centuries, his ideas about government service examinations became the standard policy of China's imperial government.

There were, of course, some flaws in the philosopher's prescriptions. For example, he was so confident that his social guidelines would restore order that he apparently gave little thought to what would happen if conflict still arose. What should a son do when his father treats him poorly? What should the people do if the ruler seems unwise or unvirtuous? These were questions that would ultimately have to be worked out.

The Analects

Because he never achieved a high government position and never saw his principles put into action, Confucius regarded himself as a failure. Little did he know that he would one day be considered the most important thinker in Chinese history!

When he died in 479 BC, Confucius had attracted only a small band of followers. However, these men were very devoted to

---

The Chinese word translated as *classic* refers to the warp thread in a weaving which holds the entire cloth together. How does this meaning apply to the role of a classic in education?

his memory. For three years after his death, they kept vigil over his grave, mourning for him as for a father. When the period of grieving was over, they began the task of spreading their teacher's ideas to the rest of China.

A major project was to record a collection of the sayings of Confucius (and some of their own) in the nine books making up the *Lun Yu* (LOON you), which means "Conversations." They are known to English-speakers as *The Analects*. These sayings became the guides for both family life and government organization in China. They continue to have an influence in modern cultures today.

Two Important Followers

Two of Confucius's best-known followers were Mengzi and Xunzi. Mengzi (known in the West by his latinized name, Mencius — Men shee ush) lived from 373BC until 288BC. That was nearly 200 years after Confucius, but he followed in his footsteps in many ways. Like "the Master," he came from the state of Lu. His ideas were recorded in a book known as *The Discourses of Mencius*.

Mencius believed that all conflict would disappear when the social ideals of the three great leaders of the Western Zhou were restored.

from *The Analects*

— Do not do to others what you do not want others to do to you.
— In education there are no class distinctions.
— It is only the wisest and the stupidest who cannot change.
— Silence is a friend who will never betray.
— The way of the gentlemen is threefold – being humane he has no anxieties, being wise he has no doubts, being brave he has no fear.
— Judge others by what you know of yourself.
— The mind of the superior man is occupied with righteousness; the mind of the inferior man is occupied with gain.
— A person of true wisdom knows what he knows and knows what he does not know.
— A man who commits a mistake without correcting it is committing another mistake.
— Don't criticize other people's faults, criticize your own.
— A true gentleman is not partial to or against anything –what is right, he will follow.
— Everything has its beauty, but not everyone sees it.
— If you know a thing, say it; if not, admit it.

Because he had great respect for intellectuals, Mencius reasoned that people who performed manual labor should be governed, and that those who worked with their minds should govern. He created a social hierarchy, ranking (of course) the scholars and officials at the top, just below the ruler, followed by the farmers. He considered craftsmen and merchants parasites, and soldiers were so low in his estimation that they were not even included in the social order.

Mencius wrote that the people had the right to remove a ruler who demonstrated a lack of virtue. He was among the first to formally state that when the king lost the "Mandate of Heaven" (as it had been described by the Zhou), it was the moral duty of the people to rebel against the government.

Xunzi (310-220 BC) was less optimistic than Mencius about human nature. His ideas appeared in a 32-chapter book known simply as *The Xunzi*. He believed that people were naturally weak (and even evil), and that they had to be forced to be good by strict laws and the threat of harsh punishment. But he also felt that, as in the days of the Western Zhou, rituals were an important means of maintaining social order.

The views of Mencius and Xunzi had an important effect on certain key leaders of the Warring States, as you'll see in the next chapter. But it was not until several centuries later that Confucius' system of moral values and responsible behavior would begin to have an impact upon Chinese culture.

Today, Chinese people all over the world celebrate Confucius' birthday — September 28. The Kong family home and cemetary in Qufu (his birthplace) as well as a Confucian temple built there have been opened to the public.

REVIEW QUESTIONS

1. What was the basic message of Daoism?
2. What did the Daoists consider an ideal ruler?
3. What was unusual about *The Zhuangzi*?
4. What does "Confucius" mean?
5. How did the family provide a solution to society's ills?
6. What is filial piety?
7. What were the five virtues of a perfect gentleman?
8. What are the Five Classics?
9. What are *The Analects*?
10. What was a kowtow?
11. Why did a typical Chinese family favor sons?
12. Who were the "hungry ghosts?"
13. Who Mencius rank at the top of the social scale, just below the emperor?
14. How did Xunzi view human nature?

PROJECTS

1. Here's a class activity. Two students are chosen to be Laozi and Confucius. They spend a day or two reading supplementary materials about the beliefs of these philosophers. Then they come to class dressed in costume (old sheets can be fashioned into Chinese robes). Their classmates then ask them a series of questions, to which they respond according to their strong personal beliefs. Questions, preferably prepared in advance, should address subjects that will draw contrary responses from the two philosophers. Here are some examples: Should there be a federal program of the arts? What should you do if grandfather's ideas are unsound? How do you explain violence in the schools? Questions that are closely related to your personal school experience would be very meaningful (and challenging). Have some fun with this one.

2. Socrates was a Greek philosopher and teacher who lived about the same time as Confucius. Find out about his beliefs and teaching techniques. Then write a comparison between Socrates and Confucius.

3. Find out more about unicorns — the

European and Chinese variety. Make a poster comparing the two.

4. Select five sayings from *The Analects*. Discuss the meaning of each one and give examples from modern times.

5. Confucianism works when everyone "knows his place" in society. Think about the effect of Confucianism on original or revolutionary thinking. What are the strengths and weaknesses of this system of ethics in a society? Write a report expressing your views.

6. Write a play about the arrangement of a marriage. This can be light and humorous. Suppose, for example, that the two chosen spouses can't stand one another! Be sure to follow the Confucian rules for matchmaking and marriage.

7. Confucius had plenty of critics. Mozi (possibly one of his students) argued that the master's emphasis on the family led to selfishness and, taken to its ultimate conclusion, to interstate warfare! Explain how this thesis might be justified.

8. Read portions of *The Tao of Pooh*, by Benjamin Hoff (Penguin Books, 1982). Choose an example in which Pooh (or Piglet or Owl or another creature of the Hundred Acre Woods) demonstrates a basic principle of Daoism.

9. Make posters of Daoist-inspired sayings, such as, "Don't Worry. Be Happy!" Post them around the hallways of your school. Then determine whether there is a relaxation of pressure and anxiety among your schoolmates. Then think about this question: at what point does it become counter-productive to "go with the flow?"

10. Using markers or paints and posterboard, make a large *yin-yang* symbol.

11. Make up your own analects.

12. Write a saying from *The Analects* on a piece of poster board. Illustrate it with cartoons or drawings of examples from every day life at school and home.

13. Make a chart comparing Confucianism and Daoism. Use the following headings: main idea; ways to achieve goals; the ideal ruler; important leaders; strengths; weaknesses.

CHAPTER 5
THE FIRST EMPEROR

(221 — 206 BC)
UNITY AT LAST

When the last Zhou king died in 256 BC, China's longest dynasty came to an end. But since the Zhou kings had little power by this time, the king's demise had little effect upon the people of China. And the battles continued, undiminished and bloodier than ever.

By the end of the 3rd century BC, the seven warring states had evolved into three "super-kingdoms," which controlled all the land in Inner China. The "big three" were the Qi in the northeast, the Chu in the Yangzi Valley to the south, and the Qin in the Wei River Valley to the west. The power-hungry rulers of these sprawling kingdoms had amassed huge armies. The Qin and the Chu, the two larger kingdoms, could put more than a million men in the battlefield. As you might expect, each ruler dreamed of defeating his rivals and taking everything for himself.

The Mighty Qin

Of the three kingdoms, the Qin would play the greatest role in Chinese his-

tory. Let's step back a few centuries to see how the Qin people rose to power. During the early years of the Western Zhou, much of the land along the Wei River had been a royal domain for raising horses. It also served as a buffer zone against the barbarians who lived further west. Gradually, the Qin, who lived in the region, began to create a strongly centralized state. After the Zhou government moved east to Luoyang, the Qin took over the territory along the Wei.

At the end of the last chapter you learned about Xunzi, the philosopher who believed that people were basically weak.

Highlights of This Chapter

The Kingdom of the Qin
Founding of the Qin Dynasty
The New Government
The Five Elements
The Long Wall
Standard Writing, Measures and Coins
Burning of the Books
The Quest for Immortality
The Terracotta Army
The Rise of Liu Bang

Many of his ideas formed the basis of a philosophy known as Legalism. Unlike Confucius, who taught that respect for others was the key factor in a harmonious society, Legalists believed that people could only be controlled by strict laws and the fear of punishment. The Qin were very much influenced by these beliefs, and they ran a very tight ship of state. In fact, when Xunzi himself visited the Qin capital in 264 BC, he wrote in his journal that the people "stood in awe" of their officials. (Perhaps "in fear" would have been more appropriate words!)

Lord Shang (Shang Yang) was an important advisor to the Qin king. He created a military aristocracy (ruling class) to replace the hereditary noble families. For him, courage in battle was the most admirable trait, and under his influence the highly disciplined soldiers of the Qin army fought with a savage vengeance. There was one particularly grisly incentive: a warrior could advance in rank by cutting off the heads of his enemies. One head was rewarded by the advancement of one degree of rank; two heads, by two ranks, and so on. Officers were also rewarded by the total number of heads their men cut off as a unit. No wonder the Qin army was described as a "killing machine."

The Qin government kept an official registry listing the names of all members of the population was well as details of birth, marriage, and place of residence. This enabled the king to keep track of his subjects and to make sure they fulfilled their obligations of military service and labor on building projects.

The people were organized into units of five households. They were required to denounce the crimes of members of their household, even something as trivial as a petty theft. If they failed to report a crime, they were held equally responsible and punished the same as the culprit — assuming he (or she) got caught. Most punishments involved hard labor or physical mutilations (ranging from the shaving of facial whiskers to cutting off the left foot). For the worst crimes, offenders were banished to the farthest reaches of the state, enslaved, or (worst of all) executed in gruesome manners — being sliced in two at the waist with a hatchet or torn apart by ropes attached to horse-drawn chariots driven in opposite directions!

A New Dynasty

In the middle of the 3rd century BC, the Qin were led by a vigorous and capable young king, Ying Zheng. He had come to the throne at the tender age of 13, and for the first seven years of his reign the kingdom was actually ruled by his chancellor (chief minister), Lu Buwei. The chancellor was the man who commissioned *The Spring and Autumn Annals.* (He was rumored to have been Zheng's real father.) When Zheng turned 20 he began ruling on his own.

Soon afterwards, an informant told the young king about a plot against him headed by Lu Buwei. Zheng immediately removed his chancellor from office and ordered him to commit suicide. (For the ancient Chinese, suicide was the only honorable option for someone who had displeased the king, and, in later years, the emperor.) Li Si became the new chief minister, and for the next twenty years he worked closely with the king to streamline the Qin government and army.

In 234 BC Zheng became the dominant player in the struggle for control of China. In a remarkably short time, his mighty army defeated the smaller kingdoms and then the two larger ones (the Chu and the Qi), swallowing them up, wrote a Chinese historian, "as a silkworm devours a mulberry leaf." Zheng showed no mercy for his enemies — he ordered the beheading of tens of thousands of prisoners, to the solemn beating of drums. Zheng was now sole ruler of Inner China. In 221 BC he founded the Qin Dynasty.

A New Title

The title of king (*Wang*) was not grand enough for Zheng. He preferred to call himself *Qin Shi Huangdi* (Chin Sher Hwang dee), meaning "The First Emperor of the Qin." By linking his name with that of the Yellow Emperor (*Huangdi*), he added status to his new dynasty, and by adding the prefix *Shi* (First), he made it clear that he expected his line to rule China for a very long time. You'll soon find out whether he got his wish.

For state occasions, Shi Huangdi wore an elegant robe of yellow silk. From this time on, yellow was to be the imperial color, and only the emperor could wear silk robes of that color. The imperial robes were embroidered with nine dragons, each having five claws. The dragon, of course, was a key figure in Chinese religious beliefs, and the five-clawed dragon (the *long*) represented the male, positive force in the universe (*yang*). So by adopting this fierce-looking creature as his "logo," the First Emperor added immeasurably to his image of power and majesty in the eyes of his subjects. The five-clawed dragon would be the imperial symbol until the end of the very last dynasty. The robes of princes were embroidered with four-clawed dragons, and those seen on high officials' robes had three.

Dragons now appeared on nearly every official building, piece of furniture, written document, and anything else connected with the emperor. Beginning with

Huangdi came to mean either "the Yellow Emperor" of simply "emperor." Eventually, the shortened form, *di*, would be used to designate an emperor.

the Han dynasty (which succeeded the Qin), the imperial coat of arms would feature a pair of dragons guarding a pearl. (The pearl is a symbol of truth, among other things.) It was said that when an emperor died, his soul was carried to the heavens on the back of a dragon.

The Imperial Government

For the first 11 years of his reign, Shi Huangdi forged the fragments of the warring states into a unified empire. He tore down the walls of rebellious cities, disarmed their former leaders, and set up a strong bureaucracy (a departmentalized form of government) that would endure for centuries to come.

The new government was led by three key advisors: the Imperial Chancellor (who was in charge of "managing" the government agencies and running public building projects), the Grand Marshall (the military commander), and the Imperial Counselor (the key advisor to the emperor). This division of authority was intended to prevent a single ambitious man from assuming too much power. (That role belonged to the emperor himself!) A

Council of the Nine Ministers was in charge of running the Imperial household. Below this highest level of government was a network of officials, who performed such tasks as keeping accounts and inspecting ongoing projects.

The key to running a large country is breaking it up into small parts and appointing people to manage each of the parts. Shi Huangdi divided his empire into 36 districts (known as commanderies), each controlled by three officials who answered directly to him. One official was a military man, and the other two were civilians.

A commanderie was further divided into counties. The people within a county lived in districts made up of groups of 1,000 families — and these were further divided into villages of 100 families. The peasants were given portions of the former nobles' lands. In return, they had to pay taxes and serve in the army whenever called upon. Each village, district, and county was ruled by local officials, who were appointed by the man in charge of the commanderie.

The First Emperor set the tone for hard work in the government. He set quotas for the weight of documents he would read and act upon each day, not resting until he finished his mountains of work. Most imperial documents were written on silk cloth, although bamboo strips were also used. One of his officials remarked that the emperor read 66 pounds of documents every day!

A Magnificent Capital

Shi Huangdi built his capital at Xianyang, on the banks of the Wei River. This site was easily defended, because it lay nestled within two mountain ranges and could only be approached from the east or the river itself. Like all ancient Chinese cities, it was surrounded by earthen walls. (The character for wall also means city.)

Each commander in the Qin army was issued a half of a special token of identification, a palm-sized tally. Because the token was usually carved in the form of a tiger, it was called a "tiger tally." The emperor had the other half of the token. To move troops, the commander had to ask for permission. The emperor signified his approval by sending him a messenger carrying his half of the tiger tally. If the two halves fitted exactly, the commander knew that the imperial consent was genuine. Tiger tallies were also sent between army commanders during military engagements. If the messenger's half tally did not match the half held by the receiving officer, the message would be rejected.

The tiger was considered the "king of beasts" in ancient China. (There were no lions in this part of the world.) The mythical White Tiger was the ruler of the west and associated with autumn. Tigers were believed to drive away evil and disease. As such, they were associated with ferocity, which helps explain why The First Emperor was also known as the Tiger of Qin.

The emperor confiscated all the metal weapons of his former foes and had them melted down. The metal was recast as twelve gigantic statues, which were placed within the city gates. (Each statue weighed 3 tons!)

The imperial palace (*A Fang*) was intended to draw attention to the emperor's great power. By the standards of those times, it was immense! The palace was built in tiers on a huge raised platform, facing the south (of course). Its several huge halls were linked by covered corridors. Ancient records describe a terrace that was so large it could seat 10,000 people.

Shi Huangdi ordered the nobles of the kingdoms he had conquered to move their households to his capital, where he could monitor their activities and cut their ties with their loyal followers at home. This involved a lot of people – 120,000 families! They settled in large wooden residences on the foothills overlooking the river. The presence of these displaced nobles added an element of grace and dignity to the new imperial court.

Over the years, the emperor had over a hundred palaces built in the Xianyang area. These were replicas of the former residences of the rulers he had defeated.

The Five Elements

Like most Chinese of his time, the First Emperor was very superstitious. His beliefs were molded by ancient folk religions and by certain principles of Daoism. Do you remember the two forces of the universe, *yin* and *yang*? *Yin* was associated with clouds, rain, the concept of femaleness, and winter — among other things. The original Chinese character for *yin* was a picture of hills and shadows. *Yang*, on the other hand, was associated with sunshine, warmth, the concept of maleness, and summer. (And, of course, the *long* dragon!) The character for *yang* was a picture of slanting sun rays. Both forces were present in everything, but one dominated — sometimes it was *yin*, sometimes *yang*.

The ancient Chinese also believed that the universe was made up of five elements — earth, wood, metal, fire, and water. Like *yin* and *yang*, these elements were interrelated; they succeeded one another in an unending cycle. Here's how it worked.

Earth was very heavy (which made it "strong"), but a wooden shovel could dig it up. So earth was "overcome" or defeated by wood. Wood, in turn, was defeated by metal, which could cut it. Metal lost to fire, which could melt it. Fire was vanquished by water, which put it out. And water was tamed by earth, which could channel and dam it. So, as you see, the elements *did* form a complete cycle.

The Daoists believed that these cycles reflected changes in human affairs. This is why the trigrams and hexagrams

Table of Correspondences of the Five Elements

	Wood	Fire	Earth	Metal	Water
Seasons	Spring	Summer	—	Autumn	Winter
Directions	East	South	Center	West	North
Numbers	Eight	Seven	Five	Nine	Six
Colors	Green	Red	Yellow	White	Black
Emotions	Anger	Joy	Love	Sorrow	Fear
Weather	Wind	Heat	Thunder	Cold	Rain
Animals	Fish	Birds	Man	Mammals	Insects

described in *The Book of Changes* were considered guides to the future. In time, a complicated system of symbols and correspondences evolved that was used to explain just about anything that happened or to predict future happenings. The basic relationship can be seen in the table above. Diviners consulted tables such as this when asked about decisions that had to be made concerning the future. If, after all sorts of calculations, a particular element was deemed favorable or "lucky" for a person (or family, or dynasty), so, too, were certain numbers, colors, and other things associated with that element.

Shi Huangdi was told that because the Zhou dynasty had been linked with the element fire, it followed logically that the Qin should be identified with the next element in the cycle, water. (This especially appealed to the emperor, since dragons were closely associated with water.) According to the ancient formulas (as you can see above), the Qin were also linked with the direction north, the number six, the emotion fear, the color black, and winter, rain, and insects. Because of this, all Qin government officials dressed entirely in black, items were arranged in groups of six, and so forth. (As with most types of fortune-telling, certain random factors seemed to add validity to the pronouncements. In this case, no one could argue with the fact that the Qin warriors instilled *fear* in the hearts of their enemies!)

New Roads and Canals

As Imperial Counselor, Li Si oversaw the construction of a network of roads covering over 4,000 miles. Five major highways, each 50 feet wide (nine lanes wide), radiated from the capital, Xianyang. They were lined with pine trees, which were planted every 30 feet. Smaller roads fanned out from the five larger ones, making it possible for messengers, soldiers, and laborers to travel to even the remotest outposts of the empire.

The roads were built to run in a straight line whenever possible. In rough terrain, mountains were tunneled through, and depressed areas were built up with rubble. In extreme cases, wooden balconies were attached to the faces of cliffs to support a narrow connecting roadway. The northern highway ran straight for about 500 miles to the Ordos Desert. (It was even known as the Straight Road.)

Because the earthen roads were easily rutted by heavy traffic, Shi Huangdi ordered that wagon axles be made to a standard size, with a diameter of 4 ½ feet and a rim of 4 inches. This allowed every wagon to travel easily along the tracks formed by the ruts.

"Water highways" also helped to link the Qin empire. The "Magic Transport Canal" was actually a system of canals dug across central China to connect the Yangzi and the West River. It opened up many miles of waterway for the transport of products, especially rice. By draining water from the marshes, it also created new farmland. This was the first canal — anywhere — to link two rivers, and it has remained in continuous use up to modern times.

The Long Wall

The greatest threat to the empire came from the bands of barbarian tribesmen who lived to the north and northwest. To defend these frontiers, the Qin linked up and fortified a number of earthen walls that had been built by various kings during the Warring States Period to form what is known in the West as the Long Wall. This solid barrier snaked its way across the rugged landscape for nearly 2,000 miles. It was not the same as the Great Wall of China that attracts tourists today. *That* wall, which lies somewhat south of the Long Wall and is

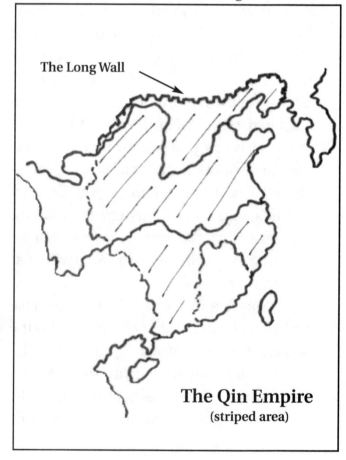

The Long Wall

The Qin Empire
(striped area)

half as long, dates mainly from the Ming dynasty, which began in the 14th century AD.

The Long Wall was built with whatever materials were most readily at hand: stones and gravel were used in the mountain regions, clay in the open plains, and layers of sand, pebbles, and tamarisk twigs along the Gobi desert. In the northeastern woodlands, planks of pine, fir and oak provided an outer casing for an earthen wall.

The Long Wall was completed in less than ten years at a great cost in terms of labor. Over a million workers (drafted from the many districts of the empire) had to be housed, clothed, and fed. Conditions were often difficult, and there were no "vacations." The men labored in the blazing summer heat of the deserts and the frigid cold on mountains that rose as much as 6,500 feet. The hours were long and the food was meager. It has been estimated that 400,000 died from exhaustion or starvation. Some were killed because they were caught napping instead of working! Others, who tried to run away, were hunted down and beaten (or executed) by overseers as a warning to others. So many bodies were buried in the wall that is has been called the largest graveyard in the world.

A Standard of Writing

The Chinese language itself posed an obstacle to the unification of the empire.

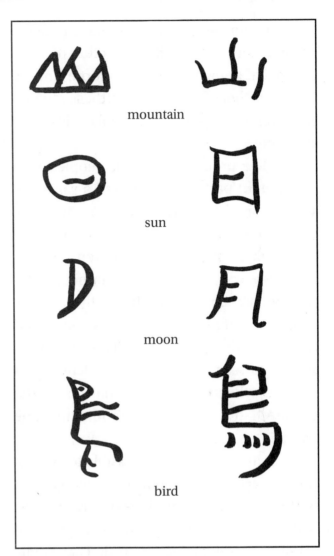

mountain

sun

moon

bird

Spoken dialects differed from place to place, and there was no single accepted way to write the language.

As you know, the earliest characters were pictures of the things they referred to, such as a house, a sleeping person, or a sack of grain. But ideas can be hard to represent with figures. Sometimes two characters were combined so that when read aloud they sounded like a concept that was difficult to represent with a single character. (Think of a rebus, such as a picture of a bee and a leaf being combined to represent the concept, "belief.") Eventually, these characters were simplified and looked less like drawings.

The problem was that people living in different parts of China used a variety of words, or characters, to mean the same thing. There was even a variation in the way common characters were written. Making matters worse, they often pronounced commonly used characters differently. Chinese is a tonal language, which makes it sound musical to English speakers. The pitch (raising or lowering) of the voice determines meaning. But the different dialects in the empire had different pitches for the same words.

Although it was impossible to change the dialects of the spoken language, the written language could be reformed and standardized. Li Si appointed a group of scholars to accomplish this task. They created a core vocabulary of about 3,000 commonly used characters and designed a standard form for writing them. Known as "Small Seal," this form of characters eliminated the regional variations. It was used for official documents as well as formal inscriptions on stone and bronze. For brush writing on silk or bamboo, a simpler form of script was developed. It was based on Small Seal but was easier and faster to write. (You might compare it to cursive.) With these reforms, the written language could be clearly understood by literate people living in any part of China.

The script created by the Qin is the direct ancestor of modern Chinese. It has not changed very much for 2,000 years. Even today, many dialects are spoken throughout China, although the official dialect is Mandarin. Yet, everyone can easily communicate through the standard written language.

Measures and Coins

The Chinese economy was also in need of standardization when the Qin united the country. Because taxes, salaries, and fines were often paid in grain and other produce, officials needed a system of weights and measures that did not vary from place to place. To meet this need, Li Si ordered the use of standard sized clay cups for measuring liquids and grains and of iron weights of similar size for balancing scales.

Shi Huangdi had accounts of his achievements carved in Small Seal script on seven stone stelae (upright tablets) along the highways and on boulders on mountain tops. One proudly announced, "Wherever the sun and moon shine, Wherever one can go by boat or by carriage, Men obey the orders and satisfy his (the sovereign's) desires…"

Two new types of round coins were also introduced — one gold and one copper. The coins had square holes in the middle so they could be threaded on a cord for safe-keeping. The round shape with a square hole became the standard for Chinese coins until modern times. (For the ancient Chinese, the round shape symbolized the heavens and the square represented the earth with its four cardinal directions.)

Don't Dare to be Different!

As you know, the Qin were avid Legalists. For them, the rules of government were what mattered most. Any sign of resistance to the laws or imperial authority led to dire consequences. Remember how neighbors were urged to spy upon one another? Even government officials lived under constant fear of "slipping up." A contemporary critic complained that punishments were so common that there were counties where it was hard to find a man who had not had a foot or hand chopped off! No doubt he exaggerated, but the image captures the harshness of the Qin regime.

The emperor insisted on order and consistency. Anything or anyone that stood out or was different was immediately suspect. Uniformity in such things as coinage and the written language were useful, but Shi Huangdi's demand for total obedience to his commands was turning China into a police state.

The Burning of the Books

The Legalist beliefs, of course, went counter to the teachings of Laozi and Confucius, and someone was bound to point out the differences between the rigid policies of the Qin and the ideal of a benevolent ruler. In 213 BC, a scholar dared to compare the emperor to the model kings of the Western Zhou described in *The Book of Documents*. Li Si, speaking for Shi Huangdi, responded that scholars who studied the past in order to criticize the present were meddlesome fools.

To avoid further criticism, the emperor ordered the burning of all "undesirable books." These included just about everything important ever written except the approved records of the Qin and certain treatises on medicine, agriculture and divination. A fire raged outside the palace gates, consuming the carefully written copies of the Confucian classics. This was followed by many other terrible bonfires.

Even discussion of the contents of the classics became a crime. Scholars who protested the emperor's actions were either forced to work on state projects or executed.

Only the emperor's guardsmen were allowed to possess weapons in civilian areas, and they kept a tight lid on any potential uprisings.

(It was said that 460 were buried alive in a common grave.) When the emperor's eldest son, Fu Su, complained about the terrible destruction, he was sent into exile on the northern frontier.

Fortunately, a few of the "dangerous" books somehow survived in the imperial library, and others were hidden by their owners. Most of the lost chapters were later rewritten from fragments found or even from memory.

The Search for Immortality

Because of his tyrannical rule, Shi Huangdi was greatly feared and generally hated. Not surprisingly, three attempts were made on his life. He survived them all unscathed, but he worried about future attacks. To strengthen his sense of security, he had many of his palaces connected by walled or roofed roads and secret passageways. He slept in a different palace every night, and ordered that anyone revealing his whereabouts be executed!

This fear of attack led to a frantic search for ways to avoid death altogether. The emperor was constantly consulting with "magicians" to discover how he could live forever. This quest for immortality was nothing new. Since earliest times, Chinese storytellers had spoken of magical places where people lived forever. Ancient myths referred to two paradises in which the laws of aging did not apply. One was the fairy domain of the Queen Mother of the West, which lay among the clouds in the Kunlun Mountains of the western frontier. In the garden of the Queen Mother grew a miraculous peach tree, whose fruit offered immortality. (The peach became a symbol for longevity.)

The other paradise was the "Island of Immortals" (*Penglai*), which was said to lie across the Eastern Sea off China's northeast coast. Here lived the Immortals — masters of time and space, who could walk among the stars and planets. They had feathers and wings, ate the precious jewels scattered along the shores of their island, and drank from the fountain of life that flowed from a high rock of jade. It was believed that ordinary humans could voyage to Penglai to drink from the fountain of life and obtain immortality. In 219 BC Shi Huangdi sent 3,000 young people on an expedition to get some of the magic potion. None of them were ever seen again, although later legends suggest that they settled in Japan.

The disappearance of the expedition made the emperor even more uneasy. The slightest suggestion of a bad omen set him off. When a large meteorite fell on China in 211 BC, someone secretly wrote on it the words, "The First Supreme Emperor will die and his lands be will be divided." In a panic, Shi Huangdi ordered the meteorite destroyed, and he put to death everyone living near where it fell.

Death of the Emperor

Shi Huangdi's last years were consumed by his worries about dying. These were not happy times for his subjects, either. The peasants groaned under the demands of serving in the army and laboring on massive projects building roads, walls, and palaces. And, of course, everyone was afraid to complain.

In 210 BC the emperor traveled to the coast of modern Shandong province to consult yet another "expert" on immortality. Ironically, while he was on this expedition he fell ill and died.

Li Si and his other ministers were so worried about the people seizing the moment to rebel against the abuses of the government that they kept the emperor's death a secret. They also needed time to prepare for the transfer of power. So they returned his body to the capital in a coffin that was carefully concealed within a "sleeping carriage." The officials accompanying the carriage handed out food and issued special edicts and imperial commands along the way, just as if the emperor were still alive. In the summer heat, the rotting corpse soon began to smell, so to disguise the stench, carts loaded with salted fish were added to the procession! In this undignified manner, the First Emperor returned to his capital.

Achieving Immortality

Shi Huangdi had intended his dynasty to last for a thousand generations, but it barely outlived him. However, his ideal of a unified empire inspired all succeeding Chinese governments for the next two millennia. (Even the name "China" is derived from Qin, which is pronounced "Chin" by English speakers.) So, in this way, he *did* achieve immortality.

Furthermore, his elaborate funeral complex proved to be one of the greatest finds of archaeological history and has made his name a familiar one among educated people throughout the modern world.

The Emperor's Tomb

The emperor had ordered the construction of his burial complex about 20 miles east of Xianyang in 246 BC. Nearly 700,000 workers and craftsmen spent 36 years working on it. They did not complete the job, since he died unexpectedly.

Once he was buried, the site of his tomb was marked by a four-sided pyramid-shaped mound of tightly packed earth covering nearly a square mile and rising 400 feet high. It was built, as you'd expect, on a north-south axis, and it was enclosed by an inner and an outer wall.

Although the tomb was declared a national monument in 1961, it has not been excavated as of this date (2001). However, records from ancient times provide us with a detailed description of his final resting place. Beneath the mound were four thick walls with gates and corner towers surrounding an underground replica of the emperor's palace. The walls of the palace were bronze. On the ceilings were depictions of the heavens — the sun, moon and stars. The Qin empire was represented on the floor, with mechanically flowing rivers of mercury (the Yangzi and Yellow rivers) draining into a sea on which floated golden boats. There was even a mechanism for operating the changing tides of the sea.

Sealed inside the burial chamber were priceless treasures. The emperor's body itself was enrobed in a funerary suit of small jade pieces sewn together with gold thread and covered with a shroud of pearl and jade.

Devices were installed that would automatically set off arrows should anyone enter the imperial tomb. To further guard the secrets of the underground palace, the workers who had constructed it were executed and buried there. (This was one of the last examples in Chinese history of mass human sacrifice.)

The Terracotta Army

A most exciting find in the tomb complex was a vast terracotta army of life-size soldiers, horses, and chariots placed in pits to guard the underground empire. (Terracotta is baked clay.) The army was discovered by a most fortunate accident in the spring of 1974. There had been no rain for a long time, and some peasants were digging a well to tap the groundwater about a half-mile east of the burial mound. They found some unusual pottery fragments, and then, digging down deeper (to about 11 feet), they unearthed the molded head of a warrior. It had not seen the light of day for more than 2,200 years!

The peasants quickly notified authorities of their remarkable find, and careful excavation of site soon began. It turned out there were four pits in an area of five and a half acres, each one 16 to 24 feet deep. To date, workers have uncovered more than 8,000 carefully molded statues of soldiers and horses.

The figures include foot soldiers, archers, charioteers, and cavalrymen. They are lightly clad for swift movement. Men and horses stand at attention in row upon

In 1980 smaller pits were discovered near the tomb complex. One contained pottery coffins with the bones of exotic birds and animals, probably from the royal zoo. Another held vessels inscribed with the words, "Belonging to the Officials in Charge of Food at Mount Li." This referred to the food sacrifices that were offered to the spirit of the dead emperor. A major find included two chariots with gold furnishings drawn by four bronze horses, harnessed in gold. Perhaps these were intended to carry the emperor to the land of the Immortals.

row of battle formation, as if awaiting the order to advance. No figure of a commander-in-chief has been found. (Probably the emperor was intended to play this role.)

The trunks of the figures were made from molds. The heads and limbs were prepared separately, with arms and legs in a variety of positions. These interchangeable parts were then assembled to create the desired model. The head was then covered with layers of fine clay in which hair, beard, eyes, mouth and muscles were carefully sculpted. Finally, small molded parts such as noses and ears (in a wide variety of shapes) were added. The facial features of the soldiers are so distinct that some archaeologists have wondered if they were portraits of actual men from the emperor's army. Some are bearded, some have moustaches, while others are clean-shaven. The men's hair is arranged in topknots, fashioned from three or six braids according to their rank. (The higher ranking men have six braids. Six, remember, was the "favorable" number of the Qin.)

Every detail of clothing was just as carefully crafted, from the rivets of armor down to the studs on an archer's shoe to stop him from slipping. The officers stand several inches taller than the common foot soldiers and have special headgear and tassels or epaulettes attached to their outer garments. After firing, a soldier's attire was painted in the colors of his section of the

Terracotta Archer

army — yellow, purple, blue, orange, green, brown, or black.

Many of the soldiers' hands were positioned to hold weapons, but most of these have disappeared. They were probably stolen when the pits were looted after the fall of the Qin dynasty. However, many bronze spears, halberds, swords, daggers, and about 1400 arrowheads remain. Some of the metal blades are still very sharp.

The first pit is the largest of the four, covering 172,000 square feet. It contains about 6,000 figures, facing east. The second pit (64,5000 square feet) contains about 1,000 warriors of the chariot and cavalry corps. The wooden chariots have disintegrated, but they left impressions in the dirt. The third pit (5,000 square feet) contains 68 high-ranking officers. The fourth pit is empty, perhaps because the emperor died before the figures could be made.

The very size and complexity of the tomb and the army is a testimony to the extraordinary management skills of the Qin. Imagine the huge numbers of men engaged in planning and laying out the complex, transporting the materials, digging the pits, creating the clay statues and chariots, and constructing the palace.

Why have the figures survived intact for all these centuries? One reason is that each pit was lined with a framework of wooden pillars and crossbeams, topped with a roof of woven matting. The roof was covered with clay. When the dynasty fell, rebels set fire to the frameworks (after looting the pits for weapons), and the intense heat baked the clay hard, thus preserving the warriors.

The Struggle for Power

Just before the emperor died, he had written a letter to his exiled son, Fu Su, saying that he (Fu Su) would soon become the new emperor. (Did he have a feeling that the end was near? We'll never know for sure.) But Zhao Gao, one of his advisors, had plans of his own, and he never sent the letter. He and Li Si preferred to have Hu Hai, the emperor's weaker second son, take the throne. (Can you explain why?) So they forged a letter from Shi Huangdi to Fu Su, demanding that he commit suicide — which he did. (As you know, it was considered honorable to take your own life if you had offended the ruler.) Hu Hai was then crowned as *Er Shi Huangdi* (The Second Emperor).

But there was trouble brewing. Zhao Gao argued with Li Si (over power, of course) and had him executed in a most grisly manner — he was cut in two at the marketplace in Xianyang. In 207 BC Zhao Gao forced the Second Emperor into retirement. (Hu Hai soon took his own life.) Then Zhao Gao was assassinated. These were bloody times, indeed! Zi Ying, Shi Huangdi's nephew, became Third Emperor. But he ruled for less than two months, before surrendering to a rebel army in 206 BC.

While all these plots and intrigues were wearing away the power of the central government, the people themselves were confused about whom to support. One thing was certain. They had had enough of

Some of the craftsmen who molded the soldiers in the clay army etched their names on the belts of the figures.

the Qin regime, with its heavy taxes, unending labor demands, and scorn for human dignity.

The Rise of Liu Bang

Amid the chaos, two leaders emerged. They couldn't have been more opposite. One was the suave and aristocratic general Xiang Yu, who championed the interests of the pre-Qin nobility. He wanted to restore and rule the former kingdom of Chu, while allowing 17 other kingdoms to exist as they had during the Eastern Zhou period. His rival was Liu Bang (lyoo bahng),

a peasant farmer who had served the Qin as a minor official in the western kingdom of Han. He wanted to restore a centralized government, with himself as emperor.

Liu Bang arrived at the pinnacle of power in an interesting way. It is said that he was ordered to bring a group of laborers to work on the emperor's tomb. When they were delayed by rain, he decided to set his prisoners free rather than face death for arriving late. Suddenly out of a job, Liu Bang joined a gang of outlaws. In time, he became actively involved with those rebelling against the Qin. His talents for

The Story of Nine Caldrons was told in later years to explain the brevity of the Qin dynasty. When floods covered China, Yu (of Xia) labored for many years to drain the excess waters from the earth. Then he mapped and measured the Nine Regions of the Middle Kingdom, collected metal from each of them, and forged Nine Sacred Caldrons. The caldrons became the symbols of royal power in ancient China. They had magical properties, and the combined weight of the nine reflected the moral worth of the ruling house. The better the ruler, the heavier the caldrons.

Over the centuries, the caldrons passed from one dynasty to another, from bad king to good king. The last monarch of the Xia was a wicked tyrant, so the caldrons were very light. He lost the caldrons to the Shang Dynasty, which ruled China for six centuries. When the Zhou defeated the Shang they took the caldrons. The moral superiority of the Zhou caused the caldrons to become so heavy that 90,000 men were required to haul each one.

When the Qin captured the caldrons from the Zhou, one flew into the Xi River. Because Shi Huangdi knew how important it was for him to own all nine caldrons, he assembled, so the story goes, an expedition to fish the ninth vessel from the water. Men in boats with long poles helped to hook it, and then very strong men tried to haul the heavy caldron out of the water with ropes. They pulled and puffed and strained. However, whenever the caldron came close to the surface, a dragon sitting inside bit through the ropes. Finally, the caldron sank to the bottom of the river and was lost forever.

leadership propelled him into the role of commander of the local rebel forces. They acknowledged him in 206 BC as King of Han.

This is when Liu Bang challenged Xiang Yu for power. After a number of skirmishes, the two men decided to join forces, but the alliance did not last. While Liu Bang had urged moderation towards the defeated Qin (sparing the royal family), Xiang Yu ordered the destruction of Xianyang and the slaughter of all of Shi Huangdi's relatives.

Do you remember how the five visible planets came together just before the fall of the Shang dynasty? On May 29, 205, the same thing happened again. It was a bad omen for the Qin.

Liu Bang and Xiang Yu fought many battles. Although Liu Bang was frequently defeated, his reputation for moderation won him the support of many of the leading generals and the loyalty of the soldiers. Finally, in 202 BC he won a decisive victory at Gaixia. Xiang Yu was captured and killed. Liu Bang promptly declared himself the new emperor of China. A glorious new age was dawning.

REVIEW QUESTIONS

1. What were the key beliefs of the Legalists?
2. How could a warrior advance in rank in Qin society?
3. What does "Shi Huangdi" mean?
4. How did Shi Huangdi organize his realm?
4. Why did the emperor insist that the nobles move to Xianyang?
5. Describe the imperial robe.
6. Who were the top officials of Shi Huangdi's government?
7. What are the Five Elements?
8. Why was the Long Wall built?
9. How was writing standardized?
10. Why did the emperor burn the books?
11. What was *Penglai*?
12. Describe the emperor's tomb.
13. Why did the terracotta army survive for so many centuries?
14. In what ways did Xiang Yu and Liu Bang differ?
15. Who became the new emperor of China?

PROJECTS

1. Historians have compared the harsh laws of Shang Yang and Shi Huangdi with those of Draco, who lived in ancient Athens. Find out more about Draco. Then compare his laws with those of the Chinese. Write a report comparing and contrasting the principles of Legalist and Draconian laws.

2. The network of roads built by the Qin empire covered 4,225 miles. This exceeded the system of roads built by the Romans two centuries later). Yet, it is the Romans that are most famous for road-building. Find out more about the Chinese and the Roman roads. Then make a chart comparing and contrasting them.

3. Write a play (it can be humorous) about Shi Huangdi's worries about death and his search for immortality.

4. During the Renaissance, there was another famous episode of book burning in Florence, Italy. Find out about the circumstances of these bonfires. Then write a short report comparing the Italian book burning with the one that took place in ancient China during the rule of Shi Huangdi.

5. Write a poem about Shi Huangdi.

6. *The Emperor and the Assassin* is an excellent film made in China about the early years of Ying Zheng, later to become Shi Huangdi. It explains the scandal that brought about the suicide of Lu Buwai. It is available in most large video rental stores. It is worthwhile watching, as it will give you a good taste of the intrigues and conflicts of Qin times.

Here's the gist of the film's plot. Lu is a wealthy merchant in the kingdom of Zhao.

He befriends Zichu, a son of a ruler of the Qin, who has been sent to Zhao as a hostage. As a sign of friendship, Lu gives the prince his favorite concubine, who is already pregnant by him (Lu).

Later Lu goes to the Qin and persuades the heir to the throne, who is childless, to accept Zichu as his successor. Not long afterwards, the Qin ruler and the heir die. So Zichu becomes king. He appoints Lu chancellor.

Zichu dies three years later. Lu becomes regent for Zichu's "son," Zheng. But Lu foolishly continues his relationship with his former concubine, who is allegedly the new king's mother. This causes the scandal that leads to Lu's suicide.

After the death of Lu, an assassin is sent from another kingdom (Yan) to kill King Zheng, but he is unsuccessful.

7. Make a clay model of a five-clawed dragon. Use pictures of dragons in books in your classroom as guides.

8. Find out more about the Terracotta Army and write a short report.

Happenings Elsewhere in the Ancient World during the Qin Dynasty

The Second Punic War, Rome against Carthage (218 - 202 BC)
Paracas Culture in Peru (700 - 200 BC)
Latin Drama Emerges with Plautus (225-184 BC)
Eratosthenes, Greek Scientist and Mathematician (276-194 BC)

CHAPTER 6
THE HAN DYNASTY
(202 BC — 220 AD)
EAST MEETS WEST

Imagine a poor peasant becoming Emperor of China! Liu Bang was living proof that a man of talent could receive the Mandate of Heaven, regardless of his origins. He called his new dynasty the Han, after his native kingdom. He built his capital at Chang'an, across the Wei river from the ruins of the Qin capital, Xianyang.

The Han ruled for nearly 400 years. During this exciting period in history, Chinese culture spread far beyond the eastern river valleys. Contact was made for the first time with the western world, preparing the way for an exchange of ideas as well as products and technology.

Today, most ethnic Chinese (those not of foreign origin) are descended from the Han. In fact, the word denoting someone Chinese is also translated "son of Han." Liu Bang is often referred to as Han Gaozu ("Forefather of Han"), just as George Washington is known as "The Father of His Country." He is known to historians as Gaodi, the name given him posthumously (after his death), Gaodi, so we'll refer to him in that way.

As with the Zhou, the Han dynasty is divided into two major periods, which take their names from the sites of the capitals. During the Western Han period, the capital was Chang'an; after a short lived interlude (the Xin dynasty), the capital was moved east to Luoyang, and the Eastern Han period began.

Highlights of This Chapter

Gaodi's new government
Empress Lu
The Jade Prince
The Tomb of Countess Dai
The Civil Service Exams
The Travels of Zhang Qian
The Silk Road
Sima Qian, Grand Historian
The Xin Dynasty
The Move to Luoyang
Ban Zhao and Ban Chao
Daoism Becomes a Religion
The Invention of Paper
Advances in Science and Farming

The Western Han
(202 BC - 8 AD)

A Gentler Government

Gaodi's first task was to reunite his empire and win the support of his subjects. By this time, many educated people had become attracted to the ideas of Confucius. These "Confucianists" had joined the rebels in fighting and ultimately toppling the Qin dynasty. Because he was illiterate, Gaodi was not very comfortable in the company of scholarly men, but he recognized the need for educated advisers. So he began working with the Confucian scholars to design his new government. He immediately abolished the harsh policies of Legalism and replaced them with a more practical and humane approach to leadership. He hoped to be the sort of benevolent ruler Confucius had envisioned.

Gaodi even sponsored a project to compile writings about principles of good government. (As you know, most of the books had perished in the flames of Shi Huangdi's bonfires.) A scholar named Lu Jia wrote *The New Analects*, which condemned the shortcomings of Legalism and reconfirmed the wisdom of Confucius.

Gaodi retained the basic structure of the Qin bureaucracy. His government was headed by three ministers, known as the Three Excellencies, who were in charge of finance, the military, and public building projects. Each minister had a staff of nine assistant ministers, who helped him implement new policies. The assistant ministers were also responsible for such matters as security, courts, the maintenance of the palace, and the reception of foreign visitors. (Diplomacy was to play a major role in government during the Han dynasty.)

The organization of the Han empire also reflected that of the Qin. Gaodi maintained the commanderies in the area around Chang'an, although he allowed ten kingdoms in the east and south to function independently as long as their rulers swore allegiance to him. Gradually, he would replace these rulers with members of his own family. The leaders of the commanderies and kingdoms were directly responsible to the top officials in Chang-an and, of course, answerable to the emperor himself.

Gaodi brought back the elaborate court rituals of the Zhou, which had been so admired by Confucius. By restoring the traditions of the beloved leaders of earlier times (remember the Duke of Zhou?), he

A Chinese scholar described Liu Bang as a man with a prominent nose, a "dragon-like" forehead, and whiskers on his chin and cheeks. Despite his great achievements, he was a poorly educated man, whose rural accent, earthy vocabulary, and rowdy behavior often shocked the upper classes!

further strengthened his claim to the throne. He also adopted the Confucian practice of kowtowing. (The kowtow, remember, involved kneeling and touching one's head to the floor to show respect for a superior authority.) From this time on, every court official and diplomat was expected to kowtow to the emperor before presenting his business.

Problems to the North

Mongolia was a rugged region of grasslands, mountains, and deserts north of Inner China. Nomads, known as the Xiongnu, lived here as herders of sheep, goats, camels, and horses. They migrated with the seasons, moving their camps to where the grazing was best — north in summer and south in winter. The Chinese army came to depend upon the tribesmen for supplies of new mounts for the cavalry.

The Xiongnu were renowned horsemen, and their ability to accurately shoot arrows while riding at a full gallop made them an awesome fighting force. From time to time, bands of Xiongnu sneaked over the border and raided villages in China. The Chinese farmers, as you would expect, hated the nomads, whom they regarded as lazy, uncouth bandits. The horsemen, on the other hand, gloried in their military skills and looked with scorn upon the farmers, whom they considered weaklings incapable of defending themselves.

In 209 BC, a charismatic leader named Maodun had created a confederacy of all the Xiongnu tribes. He established a capital at Longcheng and began expanding his territory southwards. Shi Huangdi sent 100,000 soldiers to the northern frontier in 213 BC to push the Xiongnu back. His Long Wall was intended in large part to keep these warriors out of China.

Gaodi led a large army against the Xiongnu in 200 BC, but his troops were no match for the nomads, and he narrowly escaped with his life. After this close call, he changed his policy towards the barbarians from one of aggression to one of diplomacy. He sent a Chinese princess as a bride to the Xiongnu leader as well as numerous gifts. This plan led to a mutual recognition of (and respect for) the border separating Xiongnu and Chinese territory — at least for the time being.

Able-bodied men were enrolled in the Han army for two years, and after that time they had to be ready for recall in times of emergency until they were 56. They drew their supplies of clothing and weapons from the government and were likely to serve in any part of the empire where troops were required.

The stirrup, invented around 200 BC, increased the value of the cavalry, since it enabled a rider to keep his seat on his horse while charging an opponent, throwing a weapon, or shooting an arrow.

The Empress Lu

Gaodi was killed in 195 BC during a military skirmish. For the next 16 years, the government of China was dominated by his strong-willed widow, Dowager Empress Lu Hou. (A dowager is the widow of a titled person.) Although an emperor had many mistresses, known as consorts and concubines, who bore him children, the empress ruled the harem, and her oldest son became heir to the throne.

Empress Lu had only one son, a 15-year-old boy. When he became emperor (Huidi), she made the major decisions. According to the rules of filial piety, even the emperor asked his mother for advice, and the empress certainly took every advantage of this opportunity. She seized the reins of power and wouldn't let go! To secure her position, she ordered the imprisonment (and death) of Gaodi's concubines, as well as anyone in the government who didn't agree with her.

Empress Lu chose men from her own family to rule four small eastern kingdoms, and she appointed other relatives to high government posts. She further promoted the interests of her family (and herself!) by arranging marriages between eligible Lu women and important imperial ministers.

When Huidi died in 188 BC without an heir, his mother placed another young boy on the throne. When *he* became too independent, she sent him to prison and set up a third child as emperor — one she could control as easily as Huidi.

Upon the death of the empress in 180 BC, Gaodi's three surviving sons had the entire Lu clan executed. They then chose their half-brother, Wendi, to be the next emperor — largely because his mother had no powerful relatives!

In later years, when an empress seemed to be gaining too much power, government leaders would shudder and take heed, reminding one another of the infamous Empress Lu!

A Time of Prosperity

Wendi is remembered as a model Confucian ruler. He lived frugally and worked hard to strengthen his empire and improve the lives of his subjects. For example, he organized a system for providing relief to starving peasants in times of famine and for giving pensions to the elderly. His reign (and that of his son, Jingdi) marked the beginning of a period of prosperity that would last for the rest of the Western Han period.

The public works construction projects begun by Shi Huangdi were continued during the Western Han period. The network of roads was extended west and south. Major roads as wide as 75 feet had three lanes, the paved central lane being reserved for messengers and officials (and, of course, the emperor).

But what intrigues archaeologists are the lavish tombs and burial practices that date from this time. Most famous are the tombs of the "Jade Prince," the Countess of Dai, and Emperor Jingdi. Let's take a closer look.

The Jade Prince

In 1968 archaeologists excavated the tomb of Prince Liu Sheng, who lived in a small kingdom and died in 168 BC. His remains were encased in an entire suit of jade.

Jade is a beautiful, durable stone (only a diamond is harder), which seems to glow when it is highly polished. Its color ranges from dark brownish green to very pale, greenish white. Its Chinese name (*yu*) means "the fairest of stones." Jade is most commonly found in pebbles and boulders whose rough exterior provides no clue to the beauty of the material within. Because of this, the ancient Chinese considered jade symbolic of the "inner beauty" of a person.

As you've learned, jade was shaped into objects by Chinese craftsmen from ear-liest times, and many elegant artifacts have been found in Shang and Zhou tombs. The jade could not be chipped or flaked, but had to be ground away with a metal tool patient-ly worked back and forth over a paste made from sand and grease. Because of the stone's beauty and the difficulty of working with it, jade objects were valued far above gold and other precious gems.

Han craftsmen used iron tools, which cut and shaped the jade more efficiently than the bronze tools used by the Zhou. Among the more practical items they made were character seals used for stamping doc-uments. Some of these seals have been found in tombs with traces of ink still visi-ble. Elaborately carved jade buckles and pendants were popular among those who could afford them. A Han emperor often wore a hat with nine strings of jade beads dangling from the front and back brims. In later times, an emperor would carry a jade scepter as a symbol of their power.

The hardness of jade made the stone seem indestructible. This led the Chinese to believe that jade could protect the body

---

Han scholar Xu Shen wrote in his dictionary (*Shuowen jiezi*) that jade was endowed with five Confucian virtues. Charity was reflected by its luster, bright yet warm; moral integrity by its translucen-cy, revealing the color and markings within; wisdom by the purity and penetrating quality of the note when the stone was struck; justice, since it could be broken but never bent; and equity, because it had sharp angles which caused no injury.

The Chinese describe the varying shades of jade as "apple green," "spinach green," "camphor," "old snow," "mutton fat," and "red."

from decay. Even poor people were buried with at least a small bead of jade, which served as an amulet (magic charm). Shi Huangdi was buried in a garment made of jade. But the Jade Prince, as you know, wore an entire body suit fashioned from small pieces of the precious stone.

The archaeologists who discovered Liu Sheng's tomb had their work cut out for them. The tomb had been carved into the side of a small mountain and sealed with a thick plate of molten iron. Once they got through that barrier, the archaeologists found themselves in a huge 65-foot wide entrance hall. It was bigger than a modern barn.

To the left of the hall was a vast storage chamber, filled with thousands of artifacts, including a magnificent jade disc carved with dragons. Food and drink were provided for the *po,* the part of the soul that remained with the body after death. (The ancient Chinese believed that the human soul had two parts that separated upon death. The spiritual part (the *hun*) ascended to the heavens and joined the spirits of the ancestors. The other part (the *po*) remained close to the body and had to be kept satisfied so it would not become restless and haunt surviving relatives. The ideal tomb was designed to create an environment so comfortable and familiar that the earthbound part of the soul would remain happy.) Liu Sheng had loved wine, and he

was buried with more than 1300 gallons of it. (That should have kept his *po* very satisfied!)

To the right of the huge hall was a stable containing six chariots and the skeletons of horses. Directly behind the hall was the coffin chamber, containing the bodies of the Prince and his wife, Don Wan. They were both dressed from head to toe in suits of jade, their heads resting on bronze pillows. The jacket and pants, hood, face mask, gauntlets, and boots of the Prince's suit (the

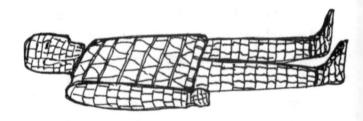

larger of the two) were fashioned from about 2,500 wafer-thin jade plaques, stitched together at the edges with over 30,000 pieces of gold wire. Special jade plugs had been inserted in the nose, ears, and mouth of the Prince and his wife, and their eyes had been covered with small jade "shields." Such attire would have taken years to make, so the royal couple must have been measured for them when they were very young adults.

The families who buried the royal

couple would have been dismayed to learn that the jade did not have the preservative power they had hoped for. The bodies had badly decomposed, and the suits themselves had fallen apart into a jumble of jade plaques and scraps of gold wire. Since this discovery, archaeologists have carefully reconstructed the pieces of Liu Sheng's jade suit. It took almost as long to reconstruct it as it had taken craftsmen to make it in the first place.

The Tomb of the Countess of Dai

The tomb of the Countess of Dai was discovered in 1972 at Mawangdui (in Hunan province). She died in the same century as Liu Sheng. However, her body was mummified (sun-dried) and then wrapped in 20 silk garments bound with silk ribbons. (When it was discovered, the body was almost perfectly preserved, so for whatever reason she chose mummification over a jade suit, she made a good choice!) The Countess lay in a nest of four coffins, one inside the other. Around the coffins were 46 rolls of fine silk cloth as well as many silk robes and cloaks. There were also 162 wooden models of servants to wait upon the Countess in her afterlife. (They were expected to come to life when the tomb was sealed.)

The most exciting find in the tomb was a silk banner on the lid of the inner coffin. It bears a three-part painting that depicts the journey of the Countess' *hun* (the part of the soul that leaves the tomb and joins the spirit world) to Heaven. On the lowest level in the painting is the dark and dreary underworld, filled with ugly demons. Above that is the earthly world, where the funeral ceremony is taking place. The Countess appears in the center, with her relations kneeling around her, calling on her *hun* to fly to the realm of the spirits. Above them floats the gate to Heaven, guarded by its faithful keeper, a giant bat. All sorts of deities and sacred creatures soar through the celestial skies. The three levels of the painting are bound together on one side by two huge dragons, their bodies coiled and entwined in perfect symmetry. This wonderfully preserved banner is the earliest known Chinese painting to have survived to our times.

Sections of the banner painting are repeated on the lids of the coffins. A winged Immortal appears on the innermost coffin to guide the countess' *hun* on its journey. The Immortal is accompanied by four animals that figured prominently in ancient mythology — the dragon, the phoenix, the deer, and the tiger. The second coffin lid features strange-looking creatures, chasing one another amid swirling clouds on a black background. These are guardian beasts, whose duty is to ward off demons and evil spirits.

A nearby tomb contained the body of

the Countess' son. Buried with it were more than 20 ancient texts written on silk, including the oldest known copy of *The Book of Changes.*

Jingdi's Army

Do you remember the Terracotta Army? Several Han rulers followed Shi Huangdi's example by burying clay armies near their final resting places. One of these "armies" was discovered in 1990 as a result of the popularity of viewing the tomb of the First Emperor. So many tourists wanted to see the famous Terracotta Army that the Chinese government had to build a new airport. A crew of laborers was in the process of building a road connecting the new airport with the tomb when their shovels unearthed the clay foot soldiers of the fifth Han emperor, Jingdi

Jingdi's troops numbered 40,000 (up to 400 soldiers were packed in each of 24 pits). The complex of pits covered an area five times that of the Terracotta Army. But his soldiers were less intimidating than those of Shi Huangdi, standing only two feet tall. And unlike the stern and disciplined troops of the First Emperor, these soldiers had gentle, often smiling expressions. Their movable wooden arms had rotted and dropped out of their shoulder sockets. And they were naked. Scraps of crumbling silk and embroidery provided clues that the little soldiers originally wore individually tailored suits of silk.

Also included in the pits were figures of domestic animals, farm tools made of bronze and iron, the remnants of wooden carts, weights and measures, and storage jars filled with real grain. These findings provide an intriguing time capsule of life in early Han times.

Wudi Begins His Long Reign

The height of the Han dynasty was the reign of Wudi, who succeeded Jingdi. He ruled an amazing 54 years (140 – 87 BC), which makes his one of the longest reigns in

Han craftsmen applied lacquer to elegant containers made of cloth, leather, metal, as well as carved wood. They were decorated with real and mythical animals, birds, and geometric patterns. The shiny, hard nature of lacquer enhanced the bright, vivid colors used, making the figures stand out sharply against the uniform background.

Laquerware made by the Han was of such extraordinary beauty that the finest objects were prized second only to jade. Most were produced in the provinces of Sichuan and Hunan in a labor-intensive and time-consuming process. Han artisans increased their output by dividing the tasks and working as a team in an early version of mass production. One craftsman prepared the form, the next applied the base coat of lacquer, another carved the design, and someone else polished the finished product.

Chinese imperial history.

Wudi strengthened the central government by further curbing the power of the nobles. Until now, the wealthy landowners had passed on their estates to their oldest sons, so the land was controlled by a small group of powerful property owners. Wudi issued a proclamation that required one half of an estate to go to the oldest son upon the death of the father, but the other half to be divided among the other sons. According to this plan, the estates would decrease in size with each new generation, thus reducing the power of individual men.

In time, Wudi saw to it that most of the kingdoms in the empire were replaced by commanderies, which were divided into counties. The county officials were in charge of registering the population, conscripting able-bodied men for service in the army or the labor gangs, collecting taxes in the form of grain, maintaining the waterways, and presiding over the local courts.

The Civil Service Exams

Like the Han emperors who preceded him, Wudi believed the key to good government was a "team" of officials well-educated in the Confucian texts. (Confucianism was now the official state philosophy.)

Beginning in 141 BC, the senior officials were required to submit the names of well-qualified candidates for government positions. Several years later, special positions were created for scholars interested in interpreting the Confucian texts.

In 124 BC Wudi founded the Imperial Academy in Chang'an. Here young men studied the *Five Classics* you've already learned about as well as *The Analects* and the collected writings of Mencius. The texts of these writings had to be memorized, word for word. It was a demanding and daunting task, but one well worth the effort. At the end of their term of study, the young men took an exam. If they passed, they became eligible for an official appointment.

The system of exams provided a way for talented men, regardless of the wealth of their families, to obtain high level jobs and the prestige that came with it. As the civil service exam system developed, entire families rose and fell in status, depending on whether or not they produced successful candidates.

Although the rich had an edge in the exams (the sons of a noble family had private tutors from an early age), the exam system made it easier for an ordinary man to move upward in society in China than anywhere else in the world. During Wudi's reign, a former swineherd named Gongsun Hong became Chancellor. Confucius would have been pleased!

The Confucian Family

As you learned earlier, Confucius considered the family the building block of a harmonious society. And since these early times, the birth of a boy was a special occasion, since a boy could carry on the family name, conduct ancestor worship, and, if the family was of high standing, maintain their social status. Although girls could help improve a family's lot by making a good marriage, they were generally viewed as something of a drain on the family resources because they needed dowries.

Parents arranged marriages for their children while they were still young. Once married, a girl transferred her allegiance from her own family to that of her husband. Although women were usually treated with indifference, the mother of many sons was honored.

Of course, an older person always had higher status than a younger one, and a male ranked above a female. A younger child always obeyed his or her older siblings, and it was common to refer to family members by their ranking, such as "Elder Sister" or "Second Son," rather than by personal names. The first son in a family had great power and influence, even more so if he was the first son of a first son. And it mattered a lot whether a cousin was the child of a second born son or first born son, just as it mattered if an uncle was from the mother's side or father's side. In fact, there was no word for uncle, only separate words meaning "father's eldest brother," "father's youngest brother," "mother's eldest brother," and so on.

Everyone was expected to follow the Confucian rules of social etiquette. Striking an older brother or sister was punishable by two years of hard labor! Hitting an older cousin had a lighter sentence – perhaps one hundred wacks with a metal rod. And anyone who lifted a hand against his parents or grandparents could be beheaded!

The Empire Expands

Wudi means "Martial Emperor," and the man certainly lived up to his name. Under his leadership, China almost doubled in size. He extended the northeastern frontier into Manchuria, founded four commanderies in northern Korea, and, further south, established commanderies in the present-day provinces of Guangdong and Guangxi, as well as in northern Vietnam.

At the age of four children began writing simple characters. At eight, they began school where they learned the core of the Confucian doctrines in rhyming, jingle form. They practiced the rhymes over and over again until they memorized passages. At the age of 15, they began more advanced studies of the Confucian canons. They learned composition and studied commentaries of the classic writings. Teachers were extremely strict and demanding. Going to school was not much fun!

The Travels of Zhang Qian

Wudi's biggest challenge was protecting his northern frontier. In 166 BC, 140,000 Xiongnu horsemen raided deep into China, reaching a point less than 100 miles from Chang'an. The emperor responded by sending troops far into Xiongnu territory, driving the nomads back to the Gobi Desert. He then strengthened the border by extending the Long Wall eastward and stationing soldiers permanently along it.

A road along the top of the wall enabled soldiers to travel quickly to any area of the frontier that was threatened. Wudi also added watchtowers to the wall. These were wider than the wall itself, and they allowed archers in them to shoot at invaders scaling the wall on ladders. Soldiers in separate watchtowers signaled one another using smoke by day and fire by night.

But the tribesmen remained a troubling presence. In 138 BC Wudi decided to seek allies among the enemies of the Xiongnu. He organized an expedition of high officials to travel westward to present-day Afghanistan to meet with the leaders of the Yuezhi. These tribesmen had been driven out of their homeland to the east by the Xiongnu. Wudi figured they would be willing to team up with him to win back some of their land.

Unfortunately, the leader of the expedition, Zhang Qian, was captured as they traveled through Xiongnu territory. He spent ten years as the prisoner of those enemy tribesmen before escaping to continue his mission. When he finally reached the Yuezhi, he discovered to his dismay that they had no desire to tangle with the Xiongnu. However, they were very interested in establishing trade relations with China.

Zhang Qian returned to Wudi's court in Chang'an 12 years after his departure. He brought with him a variety of "exotic" animal and plant specimens (including walnuts and grapevines), as well as manuscripts with "foreign" writing (probably Sanskrit). He was accompanied by his barbarian wife and only one of his original 100 followers.

Zhang Qian told the emperor about the kingdom of Ferghana (present-day Uzbekistan), where the horses were bigger than the stocky ponies bred by the Mongolian nomads. They were, in fact, large enough to carry heavily armed men at a fast pace. He also spoke about camel caravans that were transporting bamboo and silk cloth and trading them for gold. He even referred to a huge empire that lay further west. This was the mighty Roman Empire. For the first time, the Chinese learned of other civilized peoples who had developed rich cultures independently of China. It must have been a shock to learn that China might not be "the Middle Kingdom" after all.

Wudi was intrigued by the accounts of the peoples living beyond his western borders — and even more so by the horses. In 104 he sent the first of several military expeditions to this region. His soldiers crossed some of the earth's most rugged terrain and reached places over 2,000 miles from Chang'an. This in itself was an impressive achievement.

Some of his men entered Ferghana and seized entire herds of horses. The larger, more elegant steeds would become a sta-tus symbol for the wealthy Chinese, who called them "flying" or "heavenly" horses, because they seemed to fly through the air, unlike the short-legged horses from Mongolia.

Other troops defeated a force of Xiongnu and Roman soldiers. The Romans had been captured by the nomads and recruited into the Xiongnu army just before the Chinese attacked. Recently, archaeologists have discovered many clues at the site that provide a fascinating view of the only known clash between soldiers from the mighty empires of China and Rome.

The spirited horses of Ferghana have been immortalized in a bronze "flying horse" found in a Han tomb in Gansu.

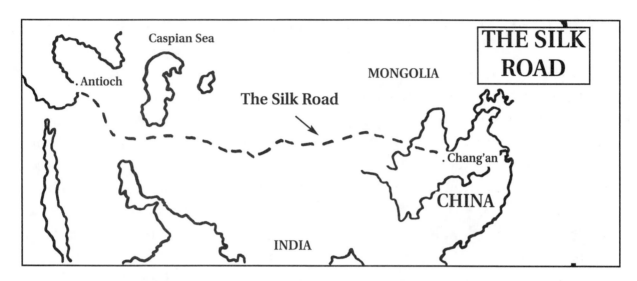

The Silk Road

The western campaigns won Wudi control of a vast trade network linking eastern and western Asia. Caravans of camels, each carrying over 400 pounds of silk cloth, were soon following in the footsteps of Zhang Qian, slowly plodding from Chang'an to Persia. For this reason, the trade route became known as the Silk Road.

The caravans traveled for months, passing through some of the most inhospitable regions in the world — rocky, snow-topped mountains and burning deserts. The Chinese called the Taklamakan Desert the "sea of death," with its shifting dunes rising up to 300 feet. The two-humped (Bactrian) camels could smell underground water in the desert, and they warned their riders of deadly, suffocating sandstorms by huddling together, snarling, and burying their faces in the sand.

The caravans faced other dangers as well — raiding horsemen who galloped from out of nowhere, poisonous snakes, disease, sunstroke, and a lack of food when supplies ran low. But the promise of a good profit lured the merchants to weather the elements. Once a caravan arrived at the end of the Silk Road in Persia (3,700 miles from Chang'an), Middle Eastern merchants bargained for the products and took them to Antioch, the capital of Syria. From there they were shipped to ports along the Mediterranean Sea. The biggest market was Rome.

The Silk Road brought about an exchange of wares previously unknown in China. Many merchants became quite wealthy, much to the dismay of members of the upper class. (As you know, merchants

The Silk Industry

As you know, silk had been a major product in China since very early times. But by the Han dynasty, techniques of sericulture (the breeding of silkworms and the weaving of silk cloth) had greatly advanced.

The silkworms were now raised on special farms. A female silkworm moth laid over 500 yellow eggs, each no bigger than the head of a pin. After hatching, the tiny silkworms were kept on wooden trays that were arranged on large cabinets like drawers. They were fed the freshly chopped leaves of white mulberry trees every few hours, day and night. The silkworms had to be protected from loud noise, vibrations, and strong smells. They were very delicate creatures!

The silkworms ate steadily, each day consuming several times their own weight in leaves. They shed their skins four times as they grew. After four to five weeks, they were about two inches long and weighed 10,000 times as much as they had when they hatched! They now began to spin cocoons to protect themselves while they pupated into moths. Each worm produced a jelly-like substance in its silk glands that hardened when it came into contact with the air. (This was silk.) It took three to four days to spin a cocoon. The single strand of silk was

were not popular in Chinese society.) Laws were passed that forbad merchants from riding horseback or wearing silk clothing. They were even required to wear a white turban to mark their undesirable status.

Chang'an was fast becoming a center of trade as well government. The marketplace was bustling , as crowds of people came to buy local products and to marvel at exotic items newly arrived from distant places.

Few traveled the entire route of the Silk Road, and most products (gold and spices as well as silk) exchanged hands several times, the price going up with each transaction.

almost a mile long! The cocoon looked like a puffy white ball.

After about nine days, the cocoons were boiled in hot water to kill the pupa and dissolve the sericin, a sticky substance that held the cocoon together. Then the silk fiber was unreeled. The strand from one cocoon was extremely fine, so about ten strands were unwoven at the same time and then wound together as a single silken thread on a wooden spool. The thread was often dyed brilliant colors.

Han women wove the silk into cloth on foot-powered looms. Over 2,000 silkworms were needed to produce one pound of cloth. Silk weaving and embroidery became organized craft industries during the Han dynasty. Imperial workshops in Chang'an and in other cities throughout the country employed thousands of women. (According to an old saying, Chinese men farmed and the women weaved.)

Bolts of raw silk were often used as currency from Zhou times through the Tang dynasty (618 - 907 AD). A pound of silk was worth a pound of gold. Large quantities of the cloth were paid as taxes, so that the emperor could present bolts of silk to his generals and top government officials.

The cloth was soft, sheer, and lightweight, yet amazingly durable. It was warm in cool weather and cool in hot weather. Silk was indeed the wonder fabric of the ancient world. Since Qin times, the emperor and his court had worn long silk robes embroidered with colorful designs and symbols.

With the opening of the Silk Road, silk cloth became the status symbol of the well-to-do living thousands of miles away from Chang'an. Wealthy Roman women were soon wearing long garments and cloaks made of silk. The Romans referred to

---

Chinese silk became popular in Rome by the time of Julius Caesar. (He died in 44 BC, about 40 years after the death of Wudi.) The Romans thought silk came from the "hair of the sea-sheep," and they referred to the embroidery that decorated the cloth as "painting done with a needle." In return for China's silk, Rome provided glassware (which the Chinese did not yet know how to make), ivory, perfume, woolen tapestries, and a good deal of gold. Roman writer Pliny complained that women's desire to wear silk was ruining the Roman Empire by causing a drain on the imperial treasury!

Only the Chinese knew how to make silk, and they wanted to keep it that way. Tussah silk, a less fine cloth made using wild rather than domesticated silkworms had been produced in India since about 1400 BC, but taking silkworm eggs out of China was against the law and punishable by death. The secret of making silk was kept in the east until the mid-6th century, when two Persian monks smuggled silkworms and mulberry seeds in bamboo cases to Byzantium at the request of Roman Emperor Justinian I. (The secret had spread to Japan in the 3rd century by concubines.)

China as the land of the *Seres* ("silk people"). Because the demand for silk was greater than China's interest in the products that the West had to offer, a tremendous amount of gold began flowing eastward. This would have important consequences in later years.

Sima Qian, Grand Historian

About 100 BC, a scholar named Sima Qian (See mah Chee ahn) completed *The Historical Records* (*Shiji* – Sher gee). This was the first major history of China, and it became the model for historians in all succeeding dynasties. (*The Book of Documents* was fairly short in comparison.)

The chronicle was started by Sima Qian's father, Sima Tan, who spent years compiling documents relating to the Han court and as well as to earlier dynasties. In 107 BC Wudi appointed Sima Qian to take over the task from his aging father. He gave him the title of Grand Historian.

The Historical Records contains 130 chapters, beginning in the mythical times of the Yellow Emperor and extending up to the reign of Wudi. The book includes a chronological narrative of major political events, building projects (it is the source of our description of Shi Huangdi's tomb), and biographies of important people.

Sima Qian fully intended to write a fact-based, objective history, quoting directly from documents and avoiding personal judgments. But sometimes such sources were not available, so he invented the dialogues and descriptions he thought fit the characters and situations. As a result, historical fact merged with fiction. He even included a few popular tales. Do you remember how Liu Bang led a rebellion to overthrow the Qin and then founded a new dynasty? According to *The Historical Records*, Liu Bang was one of two peasant laborers who were due to be executed because they were late appearing for work on the emperor's tomb. (This part is not far from the truth. But what follows comes from folklore.) The two men decided to stage a revolt against the harsh policies of the government, but they needed followers. So they scribbled the words, "Chen She (the name of the second peasant) will be king," on a piece of silk and stuffed the note into the belly of a fish that was about to be cooked. When some other peasants began to eat the fish, they found the note and assumed it was a message from the gods. News of this "divine omen" soon spread far

Most ancient Chinese myths were first written down during the Han Dynasty. The stories were drawn from ancient myths and reconstructed by Confucian scholars, who had a taste for order and balance. They took the jumble of tales and imposed on them the image of the China they knew.

and wide across the countryside, drawing thousands to join the revolt that led to the downfall of the Qin.

Sima Qian was an ardent Confucianist, and he predictably held up the "big three" of the Western Zhou as ideal rulers. On the other hand, he strongly disliked the philosopher, Zhuangzi, whom he described as selfish and narrow-minded.

But although he allowed his views to mingle among the facts, Sima Qian left a priceless record of the history and culture of very ancient China. He is said to have remarked, "Those who do not forget the past are masters of the future."

The Role of Music

As you know, music had been an important part of religious and official ceremonies and rituals for centuries, as well as a popular form of entertainment. Confucius said that harmonious sounds soothed the soul and were as important as food for the body. He also believed that music performed under the supervision of the emperor promoted harmony among the people.

With this in mind, Wudi founded the Imperial Bureau of Music (the *Yuefu*). Its functions were to collect music, to train orchestras and choirs, and to perform music at official ceremonies and for court entertainment. The *Yuefu* created archives of official and popular melodies. Thanks to these records, we know that there were four types of music played during the Han ritual ceremonies, and that these reflected the makeup of Chinese society. There was one type of music intended only for the emperor, one for lords, one for ministers, and one for lower officials. The position of the instruments also reflected these class divisions. For example, the musicians stood along four lines (making a square) for the emperor, three (an open square) for a lord, two for a minister, and only one for a lower ranking official.

Most of the instruments played in Han times had been invented in earlier dynasties. These included the gong, mouth organ, bamboo flute, cymbals, metal and stone chimes, drum, and zither (with 25 silk strings). New instruments of foreign origin arrived via the Silk Road, among them Persian lutes and angular harps. These were usually played by women.

Budget Problems

Wudi was in many ways a model emperor. (Sima Qian certainly portrayed him in this way.) However, his love of luxury led to spending sprees that fatally damaged the stability of the government. He filled his palaces with rare imports from the West and other distant places. He designed hunting parks that were microcosms (models) of his empire, complete with artificial lakes, rivers, and mountains. In the early part of reign he could well afford to live so lavishly. The economy was booming, warehouses of rice and wheat were overflowing, and his treasury was so full that it was said the strings holding the coins together were rotting from age. But his foreign ventures and military campaigns produced a great drain on his resources, and his expensive habits put him deeper "in the red."

Forced to look for new sources of income, Wudi and his advisers came up with some good strategies. They ordered the nobles to make "gifts" to the government. They made the production and sale of iron, salt, and rice wine state monopolies, which meant that the government could pocket all the profits. And they arranged that many crimes were punishable by a payment of fines. The government also bought rice and grain cheaply during periods of abundance and stored them in granaries, to be resold when they were scarce. This helped the people in times of famine, but it also benefited the government, which charged higher prices when the grains were in greater demand.

Many of these measures were so effective for raising revenue (money for the government) that they became standard procedures in later dynasties. However, they weren't sufficient to get the government out of debt. Meanwhile, the heavy taxes and constant recruitment of soldiers from the peasantry were making the lives of most of the people miserable. (We've heard of this happening before, haven't we?) Even the wealthy classes accused the emperor of being extravagant.

A crisis arose in 97 BC, when an alliance of powerful families challenged the imperial authority. The nobles were a force to reckon with, since they still maintained their own private armies and security forces. Men working for the Li family entered palace complex and attacked members of the Wei, the family of the empress. Because the Wei family had dominated the political scene for nearly 50 years, many people blamed *them* for the extravagance of the emperor and his court. Nearly every member of the Wei family was killed. In despair, the empress committed suicide.

Wudi sought refuge in the countryside. When he later returned to court, he was a changed man. Gone was his love of luxury and power. He lived rather simply for four years until he died. He was succeeded by an eight-year old son, Zhaodi. The boy's mother was a concubine, and since he was related to neither the Wei nor the Li families, no one complained about Zhaodi taking the throne.

Like the First Emperor, Wudi looked for ways to achieve immortality. He richly rewarded magicians or alchemists who offered him elixirs of longevity. He gave one such "wizard" a huge estate, 1,000 slaves, and his own eldest daughter as bride with a dowry of 10,000 pounds of gold.

Interval – the Xin Dynasty

The next several Han emperors tried to ease the drain of the treasury by avoiding expensive military ventures. But even with Wudi gone, the courtiers continued to indulge themselves with fine silken clothing and expensive trinkets. And then there were the eunuchs. Who were the eunuchs? They were men who had been castrated (had their reproductive organs removed) so that they could guard and live among the emperor's concubines without fathering any children. They also ran the imperial palace. The eunuchs were often very intelligent and well-educated men, and in later years they would gain tremendous power in the imperial government.

The Han regime was already on shaky footing when, in 1 BC, Wang Mang, a high minister, became regent for a child emperor. Ten years later, he seized the throne, declaring himself the emperor of the Xin ("New") dynasty. His dynasty only lasted 15 years (9 - 22 AD), however, and is viewed as an interlude between the Western and Eastern Han periods.

This is not to say that Wang Mang was a poor ruler. Quite the opposite is true. He supported the Confucian scholars, encouraged scientific research, and he had a number of plans to reform the government and bring stability to Chinese society. But he usually ran into roadblocks when he tried to put his ideas into action. For example, he wanted to take land from the rich and powerful and redistribute it to the poor. Although he had the support of most officials in the capital, the nobles had great influence in the provinces, and they strongly opposed any programs that limited their power or property.

Wang Mang's greatest success was in coinage. He ordered the nobles to turn in all their gold in exchange for copper coins, and then he put the gold in the imperial coffers. Upon his death in AD 23, the government treasury held 5 million ounces of gold — more than the total supply in medieval Europe. He had certainly made up for Wudi's losses!

In the end, it was nature that brought the short-lived Xin dynasty to an end. The

The Han devised an ingenious method for obtaining salt. They used derricks (rigid frameworks) to support iron drills, which workers operated to drill shafts deep into the ground to reach pools of salty water (brine). They lined the shafts with hollow bamboo pipes, lowered buckets down the shafts, then hoisted the buckets full of brine (a saltwater solution) up to the surface. The liquid was then taken to large iron pans where it was heated over furnace fires until it evaporated, leaving behind crystals. This salt mining process is carefully depicted on a relief carving found in a Han tomb.

Yellow River changed course and flooded enormous tracts of land, killing large numbers of people. Crops were destroyed, and this led to a terrible famine. The peasants blamed Wang Mang for their troubles. (Apparently they had to blame someone.) Now both the rich and the poor were against him. Many factions of rebels sprang up, known by such colorful names as the Red Eyebrows and the Green Woodsmen.

In 23 AD Wang Mang was driven from the throne. He was later slain by a rebel soldier. But although his reforms were not successful in his lifetime, many of them would serve as guidelines for later emperors.

The Eastern Han
(25 — 220 AD)

The Dynasty Recovers

After two years of violent civil war, Liu Xiu, a great grandson of Wudi, restored Han rule to China. He is known as Guang Wudi ("Illustrious Martial Emperor"). He spent ten years fighting off 11 rivals to the throne and conquering the regions of China that had drifted away from imperial rule. The experience of constant fighting was so draining for Guang Wudi that he later forbade the word "war" to be uttered in his presence.

Luoyang Becomes Capital

Because Chang'an had been destroyed during the fighting, Guang Wudi moved the capital east to Luoyang. (He had been born in that city in 4 BC.) Like some of his predecessors, he ordered the nobles to move to his capital, so he could keep an eye on them. He saw to it that they were well entertained at court and even encouraged them to compete among themselves in the lavishness of rituals and gift-giving. They were kept so busy trying to outdo one another that they had no time to start trouble outside the city.

Luoyang was rebuilt to reflect its importance as the Han capital city. The emperor built not one but five palaces to house himself and his entourage of ser-

Like his predecessor (as well as most of the nobles), Guang Wudi had a number of concubines (secondary wives). Candidates for this role were chosen from girls 13 to 20 years old of good families. They were examined for beauty, deportment, complexion, hair, and behavior. Successful girls were given a rank and appropriate title. The emperor reduced the ranks from 14 to 3, who held the titles of "honorable lady" (the top rank), "beautiful lady," and "chosen lady," each descending rank having more members.

The noblewomen had no role in the elegant court. Their world stopped at their doorsteps. They could only gaze at the streets from the watchtowers of their homes.

vants, concubines, and family members. As in earlier years, an imperial palace consisted of several buildings erected on raised terraces of rammed earth, connected by raised roofed corridors and passageways. Large wooden posts acted as the load-bearing columns for the entire structure of a building. These posts rested on stone bases positioned at regular intervals. They supported finely decorated beams and brackets that held the roof. The palace roofs were covered with baked ceramic tiles. The inner walls of the imperial buildings were whitewashed and painted with scenes of everyday life or mythical figures.

The rest of the city of Luoyang was divided into wards, which contained government offices and the homes of the wealthy officials. The homes were quite elegant. Most had two stories, with the rooms facing courtyards where the family could enjoy balmy breezes in good weather. Many of the rooms had low platforms called *kangs,* which were heated in cold weather by piping heat through their hollow bricks. These platforms were used for sitting in the daytime and sleeping at night. (The heat was produced by coal burning in metal braziers.) Windows were covered with paper, and the walls were adorned with beautiful silk hangings. The rooms were lit by oil-lamps at night. Each house had its own protective wall with a gate and watchtowers. (It was a minature version of the city wall.)

Luoyang was supplied by water pumped from the nearby river. The major streets had a raised center strip where only the emperor, his family, the nobles, and officials could walk. The peasants and craftsmen had to walk on either side. (They had to watch where they were going, since sewage also ran along the sides of the streets!)

Near the entrance to the city were two markets and a granary. Beyond these to the west were resorts for the emperor and the nobles — parks with artificial ponds, lakes stocked with fish, and hunting grounds filled with game. To the east were temples, funeral workshops, and the imperial tombs. (Guang Wudi's lavish tomb cost 1/3 of China's entire income in taxes and tribute!)

Ceramics and Porcelain

We know what the nobles' homes looked because of the ceramic models of their residences that were placed in their tombs. These models were intended to house the material spirit (*po*) of the deceased.

Clay tools and other "spirit objects"

The use of wooden frameworks means that few early buildings have survived – all that remains of great cities before 14th century AD are rammed earth foundations of walls, towers, and terraces.

provide more clues about everyday life. ("Spirit objects" — *ming qi* — were articles made specifically for tombs.) A grain silo ensured that there would be a plentiful supply of wheat. And there were plenty of figures of servants to serve the spirit of the deceased and entertainers to ward off boredom. The small model of a horse-drawn carriage pictured here was included in a nobleman's tomb so that he would not have to walk in the afterlife!

As you know, porcelain (a type of ceramic with a hard, shiny surface) was first produced by Shang artisans. During the Eastern Han period potters perfected the ancient methods by mixing kaolin (white clay) and petuntse (granules of a stone also known as feldspar) to mold vessels that were fired at a very high temperature (above 2,550 degrees Farenheit). Then they covered them with a glaze made of petuntse and ash and fired them again. The glaze produced a hard, glassy coating over the entire surface.

Containers made in this way became popular throughout China for everyday use. They were less expensive than bronze or lacquerware, stronger than ordinary pottery, and were easily made with local materials.

Schools for the Officials

Guang Wudi continued the government practices of the Western Han and promoted education for the civil service examination. (He himself had been a student at the Imperial Academy in Chang'an.) He established over 100 state institutes for training candidates for government positions at state expense. The Academy of Luoyang grew vast, drawing thousands of

students. A large percentage of officials were selected by their performance on the examinations. Intellect now counted more than noble birth in the government. This was not the case in any other part of the world at this time.

All schools conducted regular sacrifices to Confucius, regarding him as a royal ancestor. In time, the old philosopher would be worshipped as a god. Do you think he would have wanted that?

China Expands Westward

An ambitious policy of expansion began during the reign of Mingdi (57-75 AD). His brilliant general, Ban Chao, led several military campaigns against the tribesmen living beyond the western frontier. (The tribesmen had taken back land previously conquered by Wudi of the Western Han.) The Chinese Empire now covered over a million square miles. It equaled in size the Roman Empire, which it almost touched. Only Parthia stood between the two sprawling empires. (Look at the map on the next page.)

In 97 AD (under Mingdi's successor, Zhangdi), Ban Chao reached the Caspian Sea. He sent one of his officers, Gan Ying, to find out more about the Roman Empire. Unfortunately, Gan Ying traveled only as far as the Persian Gulf and then turned back. Historians believe that he was given bad directions by the Parthians. They controlled the flourishing trade between the Silk Road and Rome, and they probably feared that direct trade between the two empires would bring an end to their lucrative business. (As indeed it would.)

China did not maintain its vast size for long, however. Soon after the death of Ban Chao in 102, Central Asia began to slip from its grasp.

A Brother-Sister Act

Ban Chao had a sister, Ban Zhao, who won renown in her own right. She became ancient China's greatest woman scholar. After being widowed in her 50's, Ban Zhao took a post in the palace at Luoyang as instructress to the girls of the royal family living there. Her *Lessons for Women* was a book of moral advice for unmarried palace ladies.

She wrote about the cultivation of virtues she considered appropriate to women — humility, subservience, obedience, cleanliness, and industry. These related to the Confucian ideals of a virtuous woman through the three stages of her life — the time when she was obedient to her father, then to her husband, then to her son (after death of her husband). But the authoress added a plea for the education of women: "Only to teach men and not women — is that not ignoring the essential relationship between them?"

Her second brother, Ban Gu, spent years writing *The History of the Western Han Dynasty*, patterning it on Sima Qian's *The Historical Records*. His book was written in 100 chapters and included sections on imperial records, biographies, tables, and essays on such subjects as criminal law. Because he died before he finished the

Mingdi lectured on ancient history at the Luoyang Academy. As you might expect, his lectures attracted thousands of curious students.

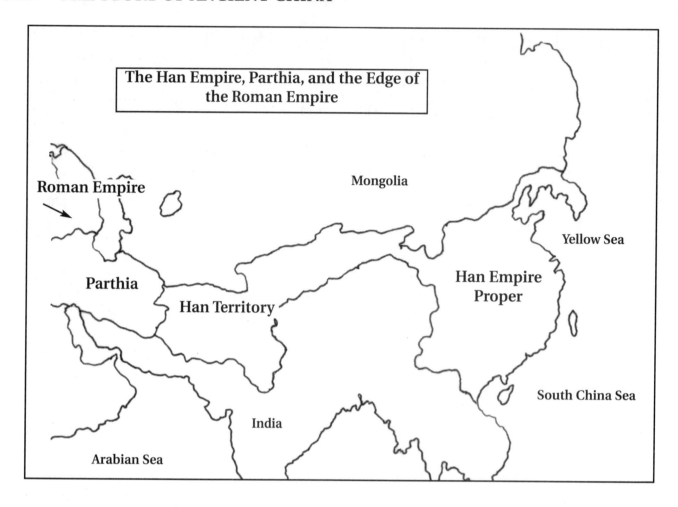

The Han Empire, Parthia, and the Edge of the Roman Empire

Roman Empire

Mongolia

Yellow Sea

Parthia

Han Empire Proper

Han Territory

South China Sea

India

Arabian Sea

work, Ban Zhao completed it for him. The book became a prototype for histories of later dynasties and helped reinforce a keen sense of history among educated Chinese.

Daoism Becomes A Religion

While Confucianism provided a system of organization and behavior for Han government and society, Daoism appealed to the people because of its emphasis upon personal freedom and its appreciation of

Ban Zhao was probably influenced by Liu Xiang (79-8 BC). This writer of the Western Han produced *Biographies of Heroic Women*, a collection of accounts of the gallant deeds and unselfish behavior of 125 women of ancient times who were notable for their loyalty to the ruler and their wise counsel to their husband or father.

nature. During the Eastern Han period, Daoism was slowly transformed from a philosophy shared only by scholars to a full-scale religion, with followers from all walks of life.

Since the days of Laozi, Daoism had absorbed many ancient superstitions and folk beliefs that had little to do with its intellectual origins. It borrowed some of the old nature gods, and came up with some gods of its own. The best known were the Jade Emperor, the Queen Mother of the West, and the Eight Immortals.

Daoists sent prayers to the Jade Emperor (Yu Huang), whom they worshipped as the ruler of the heavens. (He was associated with the beauty, durability, and magical qualities of that most precious of all Chinese stones, jade.) The Jade Emperor lived in a crystal palace and oversaw a bureaucracy (network of officials) that mirrored that of the Chinese emperor. He was one of the three "Pure Ones," the other two being Dao Zhun (who controlled the interaction between *yin* and *yang*) and Laozi (who was now considered a god).

You've already heard about the Queen Mother of the West (Xiwangmu). She was said to live in a palace of pure gold on a high summit of the Kunlun mountains that rose just beyond the western frontier. Do you remember the peaches she grew in her garden? Although anyone who ate one of these peaches would gain immortality, chances of doing this were at best slim. The trees took 3,000 years to bloom and another 3,000 years for the fruit to ripen!

The Queen Mother was usually depicted as a beautiful woman riding a white crane. (Like the peach, the crane was a symbol of longevity.) She was always accompanied by a retinue of Jade Lads and Maidens and such marvelous creatures as a nine-tailed fox, a phoenix, a three-legged bird, and a toad.

The Eight Immortals, who became very important in later centuries, were human beings who supposedly gained immortality by performing good deeds, meditating, and making sacrifices.

In the second century AD Zhang Dalong combined the elements of the pop-

The Daoists considered five mountains sacred. Most sacred was Mount Tai in Shandong province, the "Eastern Peak" where the sun rises. Shi Huangdi traveled here to make offerings to Heaven. The others were Mont Heng in Shanxi province, the northern mountain; Mount Hua in Shanxi province, the western mountain; Mount Heng in Hunan province, the southern mountain; and Mount Song in Henan province, the mountain in the center. (Remember, the ancient Chinese believed there were five directions on the earth: north, south, east, west, and center.)

ular Daoist beliefs into a formal religion, which he called the Way of the Celestial Master. He established an order of priests (both male and female), who performed rituals to please the deities and drive away evil spirits. Zhang's title of Celestial Master was passed to his son, then to his grandson, and then on to future generations. (The current Master, who resides in Taiwan, is the 64th in his lineage.)

Over the years, the number of Daoist priests grew throughout China. They were trained in special monastic centers. In time, there would be Daoist temples in every village and town. The priests' main function was to help the people achieve inner peace in this world. But the Daoists were also determined to discover the secrets of immortality.

The Quest for Immortality

The wish to live forever was, of course, nothing new. Hadn't this become the obsession of Shi Huangdi? And he wasn't the first to feel that way. Daoists had long believed an elixir could be made that would allow grant people eternal life, if they could just find the recipe.

Daoist alchemists spent long hours mixing together ground bits of metal, minerals, herbs, and even parts of animals to concoct a potion that might prove to be the elixir. (An alchemist is a person who tries to transform ordinary materials into precious ones.) Mercury, a common ingredient in their recipes, is deadly even in small amounts. So is lead. Many alchemists perished because they drank elixirs including one — or more — toxic ingredients. Traces of lead, mercury, cinnabar, and arsenic were found in the body of the Countess Dai. Perhaps they led to *her* demise.

Sometimes the alchemists made potions out of gold, reasoning that since gold retains its brilliant luster without polishing, a person who ingested it in sufficient quantities would retain his youth and never grow old and die.

Wudi had actively patronized (supported) Daoist alchemists and consumed numerous chemical substances that were supposed to bring him eternal life. They certainly didn't achieve *that* goal, but they don't seem to have harmed him. Wudi, remember, was very long-lived.

Although their quest for the magic formula was futile, the Daoists *did* discover many important physical principles. They were, in fact, China's earliest scientists. They studied the effects of potions made from herbs and woody plants on the human body and then used the results to produce medicines that were often effective. They discovered that the Chinese yam helped treat the symptoms of exhaustion, that the ginseng root diminished dizzy spells, and that mulberry wood lowered blood pressure. (Even today, nine out of ten Chinese medicines are herbal remedies.)

Many Daoists avoided foods that encouraged growth of the "three worms" — disease, aging, and death. These "unhealthy" foods included meat, alcohol, spicy dishes, and many grains. Foods most closely associated with long life were knife-shaped mushrooms (they didn't ever seem to rot or dry out), pine seeds, and walnuts.

The Energy Force

Daoists believed that a primary energy force, known as *qi* (chee), existed in both animate (living) and inanimate (non-living) objects. *Qi* was made up of the elements of *yin* and *yang*. This energy force was said to flow through the human body along 12 channels, called meridians, the most important of which passed through the vital organs. It was thought that a person became ill if the flow of *qi* was blocked.

Certain forms of physical and mental exercise were practiced to regulate the flow. Among these were techniques designed to produce breathing that was so controlled and shallow that a feather placed under the person's nose remained motionless. Breathing exercises dated back as early as the time of Mencius, who had advised proper breathing to nourish "the floodlike *qi*."

Another way to promote a healthy flow of *qi* was to practice controlled body movements. Daoists studied the ways cer-

tain animals moved when they fought (particularly the tiger, monkey, snake, and crane). From their observations they developed rhythmical exercises (known as *Tai Ji*) that mimicked these movements — in slow motion. *Tai Ji* exercises are commonly practiced today in city parks by groups of older Chinese people.

Acupuncture

Acupuncture is a technique well known in the modern world, but it was first practiced in ancient China. It involved placing fine needles at just the right points along the meridians of the body to break up blockages and restore the proper flow of *qi*. Daoist acupuncturists used charts of the meridians to determine exactly where to position their needles. The treatment often worked. Today, acupuncture is commonly used to control certain types of pain. (Modern scientists have discovered that acupuncture stimulates the production of endorphines, which are natural painkillers produced by the body as a response to pain.)

The Daoists learned a great deal about human anatomy in the process of developing their theories and charts. As early as the 2nd century BC, they understood how blood circulates through the body. (This was unknown elsewhere in the world until the 16th century AD).

Moxibustion

Moxibustion was a technique used to treat anything from snake bites to aching muscles. It involved burning a small amount of a dried herb called *moxa* (mugwort) on an acupuncture point or on the skin close to a painful area.

This practice arose after it was observed that heat relieves pain. However, the hot moxa couldn't have been comfortable, and it often caused blistering. Although moxibustion yielded fewer medical benefits than acupuncture, it did serve to cauterize areas and prevent infection.

Medical Writings

Chinese medical records date back to Shang times, when they were incised on oracle bones. The first medical treatise, *The Yellow Emperor's Inner Canon*, was written over 2,000 years ago. (The legendary Yellow Emperor was known as the "Father of Medicine" in China.)

As early as the Warring States Period, over 200 substances were used for medical treatments. They ranged from herbs to ground insects. As you've just learned, the Daoists made many useful discoveries. During Eastern Han times, Shen Nong wrote the first book that recorded medical herbs in a systematic way.

In the 2nd century, Zhang Zhongjing compiled *The Treatise on Cold Damage*, the earliest known book to relate prescribed medicines to particular illnesses. His work had a great influence on later pharmacology (the study of medicines). In the 3rd century the first book on acupuncture and moxibustion (by Mi Huangfu) would appear.

Feng Shui

The Daoists recognized that the external environment affected the inner workings of the human body. In fact, they thought of the earth as a living organism with curving channels similar to the veins and arteries through which blood pulses in a human body. Sites where these channels converged were considered especially favorable for building because they radiated *qi.*

Feng shui (fang shoo ee) is the ancient art of designing a house, a garden, or even a city in harmony with the forces of the universe. (*Feng shui* means "wind and water." The English word for this approach to arranging settings is *geomancy.*) Selecting an ideal site takes into account such factors as the positions of hills, water, vegetation, and the cardinal directions. Curved lines are preferred, because evil spirits (*sha*) travel along straight lines, and angles prevent the flow of *qi.* (This, by the way, is why the roofs of imperial and religious buildings curve upwards.)

As you know, tombs, official buildings, and cities were oriented toward the south whenever possible. This had a practical purpose, since the south was a source of a good deal of warmth. Mountains on the northern side of a site offered protection from the cold winds that blew from that direction, while water on the southern side (a river or a lake) added a cool element to counteract any excess of heat.

Before constructing a building, the Chinese called in an expert in *feng shui* to make sure it was in just the right place. He used a special compass (more about this later) and charts of *yin* and *yang*, the Five Elements, the stars, and other factors (including the location of unseen dragons and tigers) to determine the best site. Ideally, there should be just the right amount of light, darkness, dryness and water. The proportions should be 3/5 *yang* (brightness, heat, dryness, and rising forms) and 2/5 *yin* (darkness, coolness, moisture, and valley depressions). Compensations had to be made for any factors that were lacking. For example, mountains could be represented by tall trees. Certain situations, such as a house on a downward slope or facing north were unlucky, and any use of the number four was avoided, since the Chinese words for four and death sound similar.

Daoists of ancient China, of course, were great proponents of the principles of *Feng Shui*. So are many people (including modern Daoists) living in today's world. But whether or not you believe in lucky or unlucky sites, creating a balance of the natural elements *does* make for a pleasant environment.

A Blending of Ideals

Over the centuries, the principles of Daoism merged with those of Confucianism in Chinese culture. Daoism, with its stress upon feelings and spontaneity, served as a counterbalance against the logic and structure of Confucian principles. Like *yin* and *yang*, the two philosophies complemented one another, each supplying what the other lacked. And, as you'll see in the next chapter, the blending was further enriched by the arrival in China of another religion, Buddhism.

The Invention of Paper

Perhaps the greatest event of the Eastern Han was the invention of paper. As you know, the earliest books in China were made of strips of bamboo. These were bulky, awkward to use, and difficult to store, since they took up a lot of space. In the 2nd century BC, scholars began writing on rolls of silk. They were easier to carry and store, but silk was very expensive. What was needed was a cheaper material that could be easily written upon and carried about.

In 105 AD, Cai Lun, a eunuch in the imperial court in Luoyang, created a new product that met these needs. First he boiled mulberry bark, hemp rags, and old fish nets together in a large tub of water. He pounded the mixture into a mushy pulp. (The water was absorbed by the fibers, making them expand and stick together.) Then he lowered a screen into the pulp and lifted some out, letting the excess water drain out. He pressed the pulp flat to squeeze out any excess water. After the pulp dried, he had a sheet of paper. This proved to be the ideal writing material. It was cheap, portable, and could easily be mass-produced.

In a land where scholarship and writing were highly prized, paper was an instant hit. By the 3rd century AD, it was in general use throughout China. Papermakers experimented with a variety of other raw materials. They found that bamboo, rice and wheat stalks all provided suitable fibers for making paper, which then became available in a variety of textures.

Chinese Writing

As you know, ancient Chinese writing was standardized during the reign of Shi Huangdi. Let's take a closer look at the language itself. Almost all words are of one syllable. To express a more complicated meaning, two or more simple words are put together. (For example, the modern word for "magnet" is made up of three one-syllable words meaning "pull-iron-stone.")

The meaning of each character varies with its use in a particular sentence. For example, the character *sheng* (originally drawn as a small plant poking out of the earth) can be used as a verb, noun, or adjective. As a verb it can mean "to live," "to give birth," or "to be born." As a noun it can mean "life," "young man," or "student." As an adjective it can describe something as being "alive," "raw," "strange," "natural," or "lively."

sheng

A Chinese word does not change its form according to number, tense, or person as it would in English. *Ta* means he, she, or

Although fragments of paper made from raw silk from the 2nd century BC have been found in the Gobi Desert, the earliest known hemp paper with writing on it dates from around 109 AD, not long after Cai Lun's invention.

it; *ma* is horse or horses; and *zou* means go, will go, or went.

Each written character is made up of a number of brush strokes (up to 26!). They have to be drawn in a particular order. A Han scholar held his bamboo brush upright, not letting his hands or elbows touch the paper. Some calligraphers still write in this manner. (Try this with a pencil. It's not easy!)

The written Chinese language was difficult to learn, since each character had to be memorized. A scholar had to know more than 10,000 characters! This explains why, until a simplified version of the language was developed in recent times, the ability to read and write was limited to a fairly small percentage of the population.

Advances in Science

By Han times, Chinese knowledge of astronomy was impressive. As early as 200 BC the orbital times of the five visible planets (Venus, Jupiter, Mercury, Mars and Saturn) were calculated with 99 percent accuracy. (And, as you know, their conjunction was a very bad omen!)

Zhang Heng was an astronomer, mathematician and geographer who lived during the 2nd century AD. He envisioned the earth as a sphere suspended in infinite space. While he incorrectly assumed that our planet was the center of the universe and that the sun revolved around it, many of his other notions were correct. He observed, for example, that the sun was the source of the moon's light, and he explained that the moon's shadow on the earth obscured the sun, causing solar eclipses. He constructed a celestial globe to illustrate his theories. It consisted of a nest of rings modeling the horizon, the equator, the polar great circle, and the paths of the sun and moon.

In 132 AD Zhang Heng invented a device to detect earthquake activity. This was history's first seismoscope. It consisted of a round bronze vessel eight feet in diameter with a dome-shaped cover and eight bronze dragons with open jaws facing outward along the cover's rim. Each dragon held a bronze ball in its mouth. Eight toads, with open mouths tilted upward, squatted around the vessel's base. When an earth tremor occurred, a pendulum in the vessel tapped the dragon nearest the tremor, causing its jaws to open and drop its ball into the mouth of the toad directly below. This indi-

cated the direction of the earthquake.

Zhang Heng's seismoscope registered earthquakes so faint that they were unnoticed by the royal court. (In 138 AD the seismoscope detected an earth tremor 310 miles away.) This early detection gave the government a chance to send help to the disaster site before food riots broke out.

The Magnetic Compass

Early in the 1st century AD someone in China noticed that lodestone (a type of iron ore that acts like a magnet) could be used to indicate direction. This observation led to the invention of the world's first compass.

It didn't look at all like a modern compass. It consisted of a chunk of lodestone carved into the shape of a ladle and placed on a stone board with a smooth, polished surface. The ladle slowly swiveled until its handle pointed south. (The heavier part of the ladle was attracted to the magnetic north.) This early compass, called a *sinan*, was described in a book written in 80 AD. However, similar devices might have existed centuries earlier.

The compass was used by *feng shui* experts to locate favorable (south-facing) sites for tombs, buildings, and cities. It was not until later times that it became a navigational device for sailing on the high seas.

Wind Zithers

Kites have been flown in China since about 400 BC. According to legend, Kongshu Pan (the god of craftsmen) built the first kites in the shapes of birds. They had bamboo frames that were covered with silk. The earliest kites were intended to carry messages to the heavenly spirits, such as pleas for rain or for a bountiful harvest. Daoists meditated as they flew kites, and some hardy souls were also said to ride the "hard wind" on kite-like structures — they were history's first wind surfers!

Kites became lighter and more elaborate once paper was invented. They were often used to send messages and ask for help during military campaigns. Han soldiers often attached bamboo pipes to them. As the kites flew, the wind passed through the pipes, causing an eerie whistling sound. The noise spooked the enemy troops, causing them to flee in panic. Even today, the Chinese call a kite a *feng zhen* ("wind zither"), because of the sound made by the wind passing through the bamboo frame.

Innovations on the Farm

By the 2nd century AD there were about 60 million Chinese people. Nearly 90 percent of these lived in the countryside as farmers. The most thickly populated regions included the fertile valleys of the Yellow River and the Huai River (just south of the Yellow), as well as the southwestern region of Sichuan , which was watered by four tributaries of the Yangzi. (Sichuan means "four rivers.")

Most labor was supplied by humans, with the aid of a few oxen. In the 1st century a small number of horses (the Mongolian breeds, not the "flying horses") began to be pressed into duty in the fields, thanks to the invention of the horse collar harness. This device enabled the animal to pull a heavy plow without choking. Water power was tapped, too. Mills were built beside fast flowing rivers to take advantage of the force of the water to grind wheat into flour.

The wheelbarrow was probably invented around 100 AD to transport grain and farming supplies. Traders soon found the device ideal for carrying products to market, and, once there, they used the barrow as a stall. When someone designed a model with a large central wheel that could bear heavy weights, the wheelbarrow became a major form of transport, pushed along by muscle power.

Spirit Roads

Stone carvings are usually common forms of art in the early stages of development of a civilization. But this was not the case in ancient China. It was not until Eastern Han times that sculptors began making impressive stone statues. These were used to line the paths leading to imperial tombs. The endurance and permanence of the stone was associated with the immortality of the human soul.

The 1st century AD saw the invention of wooden rudders that were hinged to the back of a ship below the waterline and could swing left and right. When a sailor turned the rudder, it created enough water resistance to change the boat's direction. From Han times, sea routes took Chinese traders to Vietnam and later to Korea and Japan.)

The formal avenues of stone monuments and figures leading to the tombs of the Eastern Han emperors are known as "spirit roads." Pairs of carved stone towers (*que*) marked the start of such a road. These were carved with strips of relief figures resembling modern cartoon strips that illustrated well-known legends and historical events related to the person buried in the tomb.

Statues of huge winged lions with square jaws and massive, vigorous bodies were placed along the roads to ward off evil demons. Other mythical creatures such as the *qilin* (the Chinese unicorn) and the *tianlu* (a type of deer) were commonly sculpted for the spirit roads, as were statues of officials (which symbolized good government).

The Fall of the Han

Power struggles plagued the last century of Han rule. The rulers were weak, and the families of the imperial concubines fought with one another for power. And then there were the eunuchs. These men had become increasingly involved in high-level intrigues. In 168 a faction of eunuchs actually controlled the court. The mighty Han dynasty was on the wane.

Zhang Jue was a traveling magician, who claimed that the emperor had lost the Mandate of Heaven. He went from city to city preaching about the coming of a new regime of peace and equality that would be led by a Daoist god. He amassed 360,000 followers to rebel against the emperor. Because his followers wrapped their heads in yellow cloths, they were known as the "Yellow Turbans."

The cost of fighting these rebels further weakened the government. And there was the recurrent problem of the barbarian tribesmen, who kept crossing the Han borders. Generals assigned to deal with these problems became stronger than the emperor himself. Soon they were fighting among themselves for supremacy of command. China was once again in the throes of civil war.

By 205 a general named Cao Cao (the adopted son of a eunuch) held the reins of power as "protector" of the emperor Xiandi, who was little more than his prisoner. For many years Cao Cao ruled all of China north of the Yangzi. After he died in 220, his son Cao Pei forced the abdication of Xiandi and claimed the Mandate of Heaven for himself. The Han Dynasty had come to an end.

Review Questions

1. Why is the Chinese word for someone Chinese translated as "son of Han?"

2. In what ways did Gaodi's new government resemble that of Shi Huangdi?

3. Why were the Xiongnu considered such a threat to the Chinese?

4. Why did government officials later cringe when they heard the story of Empress Lu?

5. Why was Liu Sheng buried in a suit of jade?

6. Describe the banner on the coffin of the Countess of Dai.

7. Compare Jingdi's tomb army to the Terracotta Army of Shi Huangdi.

8. How did young men prepare for the Civil Service Examination under Wudi?

9. What was the most important result of Zhang Qian's trip to the west?

10. Why was silk so highly prized?

11. How accurate was Sima Qian's history book? Explain.

12. How did the court music of the Western Han reflect the makeup of society?

13. How could the Daoist quest for immortality be dangerous?

14. What was *qi*?

15. What was the purpose of acupuncture?

16. What are some of the principles of *Feng Shui*?

17. What was the main cause of Wudi's downfall?

18. What did Wang Mang contribute to Chinese government?

19. What was the capital of the Eastern Han?

20. Why did Ban Chao not make it to the Roman Empire?

21. How did Cai Lun make paper?

22. What is the legacy of Ban Zhao?

23. How accurate was Zhang Heng's seismoscope.?

24. What was the use of the early compass?

25. What was a spirit road?

26. Who forced the abdication of the last Han emperor?

Projects

1. The Xiongnu may have been the ancestors of the Huns, "barbarians" who invaded the Roman Empire five centuries after they tangled with Wudi. Find out about the Huns. Write a paper comparing their invasion of the Roman Empire with the Xiongnu attacks upon China. Or make a chart comparing and contrasting the two.

2. Find out more about the history of horses. Then make a poster illustrating the evolution of the horse from earliest times and the spread of the equine species from America (where they originated) to Asia and Europe. Place special emphasis upon the horses from Mongolia and Ferghana.

3. China was still the world's leading silk producer at the end of the 20th century, its raw silk production being 60% of the world's total. Learn more about the modern techniques used in China to produce silk. How much have they changed since ancient times? Make a poster to illustrate the production of silk, showing the stages from silkworm egg to finished cloth.

4. Learn more about bactrian camels. Then make a poster to illustrate your findings.

5. Here's something to think about. Because the Han dynasty was contemporary with the Roman Empire, it has often been compared to it. At its peak, the Han dynasty equaled the Romans in brilliance and military power. Hans and Romans both had strong governments that expanded geographically, promoted assimilation, and brought centuries of stability to the central regions. Both managed to deal with enormous problems of scale, ruling roughly similar numbers of people over roughly similar expanses of land. Both developed bureaucratic governments, staffing them with educated landowners. Both invested in the construction of roads, defensive walls, and waterworks. Both were threatened by barbarians at their frontiers and often used barbarian tribal units as military auxiliaries. But, of course, there were major differences between these two ancient civilizations. Find out more about the Roman Empire, and see if you can discover what they were.

6. Learn more about Herodotus (the father of ancient Greek history). Then write a report comparing him with Sima Qian (the father of Chinese history).

7. Find out more about the geographical environment of the Silk Road. Then, using clay or instant papier mache and a large piece of cardboard or poster board, make a relief map. Indicate major mountain ranges and deserts, as well as any important sources of water.

8. You've learned about the cyclical approach the Chinese took to history. A dynasty lasted until the ruler lost the Mandate of Heaven and was replaced by someone else, who started a new dynasty. Western historians tend to view history as progressing in a straight line, rather than simply repeating itself again and again. Which view do you think is most realistic? Why? Write a paper expressing your opinons.

9. During the Western Han period, jade amulets placed in the mouth of the deceased before burial often took the form of a cicada, which symbolized the continuance of life after death. The cicada has a 15-year life cycle. It buries itself in the ground and emerges 15 years later, leaving behind its dried skin (much like a snake). The ancient Chinese observed this and noted that the creature seemed to come back to life from the grave. The ancient Egyptians considered the dung beetle a symbol of rebirth. Find out why. Then write a short report describing the symbolism of these two insects in the ancient world. Include illustrations.

10. Look at the illustrations of houses of the Han dynasty in the books in your classroom or library. Make a model of the home of a wealthy member of Han society.

11. Consult some books about the modern practice of Feng Shui. Make a poster to demonstrate examples of favorable and unfavorable sites. Then present it to your classmates.

12. The ancient Egyptians believed that a person had three souls — a *ka*, a *ba*, and an *akh*. When he died, one stayed in the tomb with the body, another visited the land of the living, and the third traveled to the heavens to live with the gods. Find out more about this aspect of Egyptian religion. Then write a report comparing it to the Chinese concept of the *po* and the *hun*.

13. Ancient peoples of the Middle East spoke about a bird called the phoenix, of which there was only ever one. When it grew old, it built itself a nest of cassia twigs and frankincense and burst into flames. From the heart of this fire it was reborn. This "myth" was passed on to the ancient Greeks. How did this phoenix differ from the Chinese bird of the same name? Make a poster illustrating the attributes of the se two Middle Eastern and Chinese mythical birds.

14. Write a poem about Empress Lu.

15. Make a timeline of the major events of Han dynasty.

Happenings Elsewhere In the Ancient World During the Han Dynasty

Third Punic War, Rome vs. Carthage (149 - 146 BC)

Hohokum culture established in North America (c 100 BC)

Julius Caesar is assassinated (44 BC)

Battle of Actium - Octavian defeats Antony and Cleopatra (31 BC)

Augustus rules Rome (27 BC - 14 AD)

Life of Jesus (4 BC? – 29 AD)

City of Teotihuacan built in Central America (50 AD)

CHAPTER 7

THE AGE OF DIVISION

(220 — 589)
WARLORDS, POETS, AND MONKS

The fall of the Han dynasty was followed by three and a half centuries of internal warfare. Apart from one brief interlude, no single dynasty ruled all of China during this time. The country was fragmented, with boundaries constantly changing. No wonder this is known as the Age of Division.

As with the Zhou and Han dynasties, historians have ordered this chaotic era into distinct parts. During the first part, Inner China was divided into three kingdoms. (This is known as the Period of the Three Kingdoms.) The short-lived Western Jin dynasty dominated the second part. (This, of course, is the Period of the Western Jin.) During the third, China was divided between the north and the south. (This is known as the Period of Disunion.) Unity was finally restored with the Sui Dynasty in 581.

This could be a very confusing chapter, but we'll follow the example of the historians and move very slowly, concentrating on one time period at a time. You will discover that amid the turbulence of the age some wonderful things happened that would greatly enrich the culture of China. Let's begin with the Period of the Three Kingdoms.

The Three Kingdoms

After Cao Pei toppled the Han dynasty in 220, he founded the kingdom of Wei. It was ruled from the old Han capital, Luoyang. The following year, warlord Liu Bei (a descendant of the Han royal family) established the Shu kingdom to the southwest in Sichuan. His capital was Chengdu. Further south, general Sun Quan founded the Wu kingdom, with a capital at Nanjing. Find these three kingdoms on the map on the next page.

Highlights of This Chapter

The Three Kingdoms
The Western Jin Dynasty
Foreign Rule in the North
Chinese Rule in the South
Poetry and Calligraphy
The Rise of Buddhism
Buddhism Arrives in China
The Sui Unite China

Each of the rulers of these kingdoms claimed the Mandate of Heaven and tried to defeat his two rivals. As in the earlier Period of the Warring States, the patterns of everyday life were disrupted by the fighting. The civil service exams were abandoned and trade was reduced to a standstill. Copper coins became scarce, because some people hoarded them while others melted them down for weapons. It seemed as though all the great accomplishments of the Han dynasty would become just a distant memory.

Fact and Fiction

But although peace was elusive, this was a most colorful period in Chinese history. Some people regard it as a romantic age of chivalry and heroism, when bands of outlaws roamed across the countryside, while swash-buckling heroes looked for a chance to fight to the death for their ideals.

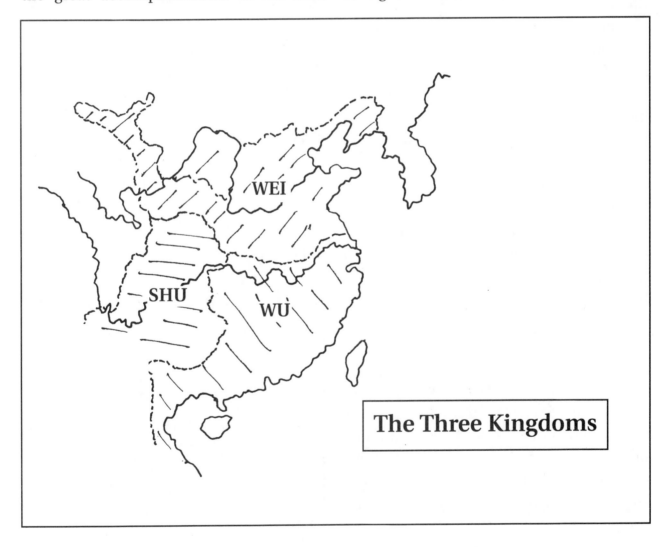

The Three Kingdoms

Storytellers living in later centuries loved to describe the adventures of the leading characters of the era. As these stories were told again and again, they evolved into a series of folk tales in which real people were transformed into popular superheroes or despised archvillains. The stories were gathered together in a 14th century novel, *The Romance of the Three Kingdoms*, by Lo Guanzhong. The book added such fuel to the popularity of the characters that they became household names throughout China. Even today, well-known episodes from Lo's novel are often performed at the Beijing Opera.

As you learned at the end of the last chapter, Cao Cao was the leader of the rebellion against the Eastern Han. Thanks to the ancient storytellers, Cao Cao has been immortalized as a self-centered bully. In one scene in Lu's novel, he slays his host because of a misunderstanding, then glibly remarks, "I would sooner betray the whole world than let the world betray me."

Tall, handsome Liu Bei (Shu founder) and his loyal companions, Guan Yu and Zhang Fei, supposedly took the "Peach Orchard Oath" of loyalty, becoming blood brothers and swearing to defend each other to the death. (Do you remember the peach orchard of the Queen of the West? Can you explain the symbolism of the "Peach Orchard Oath?") Guan Yu is often depicted as a nine-foot giant with a bright red face with a forked beard. While in reality he was a sly (and perhaps immoral) general who fought for both the Wei and the Shu, he became known as an ardent defender of the weak and oppressed. (During the Ming dynasty (1368-1644) he would be worshipped as Guandi, the god of war.)

Liu Bei's scholarly minister, Zhuge Liang, came to symbolize political cunning and diplomacy, while Wu founder Sun Quan was celebrated for his unbridled courage.

Poets Among the Warriors

Let's return to the actual history. Cao Cao as well as his two sons, Cao Pei and Cao Zhi, had talents beyond politics and warfare. They were also gifted poets. Each experimented with lyric verses of five syllables, a style that would become very important in later centuries. So there were indeed glimmers of creativity amid the chaos of the times.

The best-known poets of this period were the Seven Sages of the Bamboo Grove. They were a group of scholars who fled the Wei imperial court and met in the bamboo groves north of Luoyang. Here they played music, composed and recited poetry, and engaged in what they called "pure conversation" (discussing such concepts as truth or beauty). They scoffed at society and sought freedom of expression in the world of nature.

The Seven Sages are known as much

for their aversion to public office and their eccentric behavior as for their writings. They felt their superior gifts placed them above everyone else. The most famous of the group, Ruan Ji, responded to a criticism of his behavior with the words, "Surely you do not mean to suggest that the rules of propriety apply to *me*?"

And, of course, the wine flowed liberally. Liu Lang (always accompanied by a servant carrying a bottle of wine and a spade with which to dig his grave!) remarked that to a drunken man the "affairs of this world appear as so much duckweed in a river."

The Wei Take Over

Of the three kingdoms, the Wei was easily the most powerful. It controlled the rich farming area that made up the heartland of China and had more than twice the population of either of the other two kingdoms.

The Wei leaders built up a strongly disciplined army of mounted archers and foot soldiers. Since military might was what mattered most, they created a distinct class of warriors. Members could only marry within the class, and they were expected to produce new generations of professional soldiers.

Worried about the growing threat of the Wei, Zhuge Liang, the top official of the Shu, made an alliance with the Wu for mutual defense. But to no avail. In 263, the Wei army crossed through a remote mountainous region in Sichuan and staged a surprise attack. The Shu immediately surrendered and their territory was absorbed by the Wei. Now there were only two kingdoms — the larger-than-ever Wei and the diminutive Wu. (The Wu leaders must have been trembling in their boots!)

The Western Jin

Two years later, a Wei general named Sima Yan formed a conspiracy and forced the Wei ruler to abdicate in his favor. He then founded the Western Jin dynasty. This marks the beginning of the second part of the Age of Division.

A Temporary Peace

Sima Yan easily defeated the Wu in 280. Inner China was once again united, with its capital at Luoyang. But could the glories of the Han Dynasty be recaptured by the Western Jin? For a short time it seemed possible.

The new ruler set up his court at Luoyang and began receiving envoys from

The umbrella was invented in the fourth century in southern China. It was used by both men and women to keep out the sun as well as the raindrops. The first umbrellas were made of heavy oiled paper derived from mulberry tree bark.

distant places. In 284, representatives arrived bearing gifts from the distant Roman Empire. A most promising sign of the times was the establishment of a new academy to train young nobles for top government positions. Sima Yan had a keen interest in scholarship and collected an imperial library of over 30,000 books in Luoyang. Pei Xiu, his Minister of Works, was the first cartographer (mapmaker) to use a grid-system, drawing maps on a scale of 125 miles to 1 inch.

To improve communications among his subjects, Sima Yan built a pontoon bridge over the Yellow River.

The Fall of the Western Jin

Unfortunately, peace in China was to be short-lived. Sima Yan made three tragic mistakes. The first was to allow nomadic tribesmen, including the Xiongnu, to settle inside the Long Wall. He certainly couldn't count on *their* loyalty if the going got rough. Second, he rewarded his closest allies with huge estates. Before long, these men became powerful landowners, who recruited the local peasants to form their private armies. We've seen this happen before, haven't we? Third, he gave each of his 25 sons a principality.

As soon as Sima Yan died, his sons began fighting with each other for power. Many of the wealthy landowners joined in the fray, taking sides with whomever promised them the greatest rewards. When the heir to the throne turned to the Xiongnu for support (a big mistake!), the tribesmen took the opportunity to gain a firmer foothold in China.

In 304 AD, Liu Yuan, a Xiongnu chieftain, declared himself the new king of Han. He easily conquered most of northern China, then captured Sima Yan's successor and sacked Luoyang. The Western Jin dynasty was no more.

The Era of Disunion

With the tribesmen in control of the north, the Chinese fled south to the Yangzi River valley. A minor prince gathered together what remained of the court and declared himself founder of yet another dynasty, the Eastern Jin, with a capital at Nanjing. (*Nanjing* literally means "southern capital.")

Thus began the Period of Disunion, the third part of the Age of Division. Disunion amid division — what confusion!

The immigrant farmers from the north learned to grow rice instead of the wheat and millet that were the staples of the Yellow River region. They also learned to grow tea — a shrub with broad leaves and fragrant white flowers. They dried and then crumbled the leaves to produce what would become China's national drink. The earliest surviving references to drinking tea were written in the 3rd century.

Was China fated to remain in shambles? Many must have thought so.

Inner China was cut in two. A succession of non-Chinese rulers held the north, while five different Chinese dynasties (known as the Southern Dynasties) would govern, one after the other, in the south.

Foreign Rule in the North

For much of this period, the north was far more unstable than the south. It was often split into many kingdoms, as non-Chinese peoples like the Xiongnu, Mongols, and Tibetans waged endless wars for control of territory.

More peaceful times began in 386, when the Tuoba, tribesmen from the northwest, established the Northern Wei dynasty. The Tuoba reunified northern China and built a capital at Datong. The Tuoba leaders were impressed by many of the Chinese political and cultural traditions and adopted them as their own. This proved the key to stability in the north.

A century later, the Tuoba established a new capital amid the ruins of Luoyang. In a short time, this city grew to become a magnificent showplace of vast palaces and elegant mansions — with a population of half a million. The Northern Wei now spoke only Chinese in their court, wore Chinese clothing, took Chinese names, and intermarried with Chinese families.

Chinese Rule in the South

The Southern Dynasties considered themselves the guardians of Chinese civilization. After the sacking of Luoyang in 311, over a million people had deserted their homes and moved south to the Yangzi valley. Among them were wealthy landowners, who took along their riches as well as the thousands of people who worked for them. They settled on the best land around the new southern capital (Nanjing). Here they built impressive manors, surrounded by fruit plantations, bamboo groves, and parks stocked with exotic animals. Many of these wealthy immigrants were given high posts in the government and the army. They helped create a new imperial court.

The streets of Nanjing were soon bustling with merchants as the economy began to prosper. The south would gradually overtake the north in political, economic, and cultural importance. Even now, art and literature were about to take off in new directions.

The Scholars Turn Inward

With the fall of the Han dynasty, Confucianism had lost its popularity among the educated men in Chinese society. Its scheme of social hierarchy, which was supposed to ensure a stable government, had failed to prevent anarchy. Daoism, on the other hand, with its emphasis upon individual freedom and a love of nature, grew in popularity, particularly now with the heart of China relocated in the pleasant wooded hills and fertile green valleys of the Yangzi.

In these changing times, many scholars turned away from political matters and thought about ways to achieve inner peace. (Perhaps they were inspired by the Seven Sages of the Bamboo Grove.) Some devoted themselves to a study of Daoist writings. Others turned to lyric poetry, calligraphy, or playing the lute. A few tried their hand at painting. Tao Qian was an official who retired from office to pursue a quiet literary life on his new estate. He remarked, with a sigh of relief, "Too long have I been caught in the dusty net."

Poetry Among the Elite

With this new emphasis upon the creative arts, many of the wealthy estates around Nanjing became beacons of culture, attracting poets, painters, scholars, musicians, and even dancers. Writing verses became such a popular pastime among the elite that it became a sort of party game at banquets. The host would begin by reciting a line of verse and then challenge his guests to compose lines to complete the poem, following certain rules of rhyme, length, and meter.

The poetry of the times focused, as you might expect, on pleasant images of country life and a celebration of the grandeur of nature. The southerners had great contempt for the Chinese who stayed in the north and lived under "barbarian" rule. They considered their own poetry representative of true Chinese culture and dismissed anything written in the north as little more than "the braying of donkeys and the barking of dogs."

The Rise of Buddhism

With its emphasis upon nature and its disdain for worldly power, Daoism helped to prepare the way for Buddhism. This religion had its origin in India and was

Even the process of writing down characters was influenced by the changing attitudes in the south. Wang Xizhi was a scholar who developed a fluid "running script" style of calligraphy. His characters contrasted dramatically with the square, clearly defined Han Confucian script. He is also famous for writing in an elegant cursive form of script ("grass style") described as "light as a floating cloud, vigorous as a startled dragon." Thanks to his efforts, calligraphy (beautiful writing) was raised to one of the highest of all the arts.

In 353 Wang wrote *The Preface to the Orchid Pavillion Collection* (of poetry). This celebrated piece of writing is considered one of the great masterpieces of Chinese calligraphy. It earned Wang the title of "Sacred Calligrapher," by which he has been known ever since.

brought to China by way of the Silk Route.

Buddhism was based on the teachings of Prince Siddhartha (sid hearth ah) Gautama (Gow Tah ma), who lived in the 5th century BC. He grew up in a beautiful marble palace in northern India. Despite his material comforts, he wondered about what lay outside the palace walls.

Many stories have been told about how the prince discovered a new approach to living. One describes how, as a young man, he had a dream in which he made four nightly visits to the outside world. On the first night he met an old man leaning on a staff. He asked the man why he looked so weak and tired. "Haven't you ever seen old age?" the man asked in response. The prince hadn't, and he returned home puzzled. The second night, he passed a house where a man lay propped up in bed, shivering and moaning. When he asked him why he was in such a state, the man responded, "Haven't you ever seen sickness?" The prince hadn't, and he returned home worried. The third night he passed a man lying very still and completely wrapped in cloth. When he posed his question, he heard this reply: "Haven't you ever seen a dead person before?" The prince returned home confused. The fourth night he met a man in rags — he looked as though he was starving, and he had shaved off all his hair. He held an empty bowl to the prince. "What do you want, and why are you wearing such tat-

tered cloths?" asked the prince. "Haven't you ever seen poverty before?" was the reply. The prince returned home very upset.

So ended his dream. When he awoke, the prince began to wonder, "How can I live in luxury and comfort when the world is filled with misery?" One night he rode out into the countryside. He spent days thinking about the suffering he had seen in his dream and pondering what could be done to end it. While sitting under a bodhi tree (a sort of fig tree), the answer came to him. He had been enlightened. (To be enlightened is to be taught something new.) Since that moment he has been known as Buddha, which means "Enlightened One."

Buddha's Teachings

What had he learned? The message can be summed up in what are known as the Four Noble Truths: 1) that life is filled with suffering; 2) that suffering is caused by a love of material things; 3) that the suffering can end; and 4) that release from suffering comes from leading a disciplined and moral life and by meditating.

At the time the prince lived, most Indians believed that people lived, died, and were reborn in an endless cycle. (This is known as reincarnation.) Whether someone was reborn as a wealthy person or a beggar — or even as a lowly insect — depended upon his personal history of good and bad deeds (known as his *karma*). Buddha said that a person could break the chain of endless birth and rebirth and (by practicing the Fourth Noble Truth) escape to *Nirvana*, which was a state of nothingness where suffering did not exist. He devoted the rest of his life to wandering about teaching what he had learned. He died at the age of 80.

Branches of Buddhism

Not long after Buddha's death, many legends of his life (and even his past lives) were spread throughout much of India, and a religious cult, Buddhism, began to grow. The religion later divided into two main branches, Therevada and Mahayana.

The Theravada thought of Buddha as a historical figure. They believed that enlightenment could only be realized by giving up one's ordinary life and family and becoming a monk or nun.

The Mahayana believed in not one but many Buddhas, including one of the future (called Maitreya), who would some day come to the earth and purify it. They believed that every person could become enlightened without renouncing ordinary life. This is not to say, however, that there

were not Mahayana monks and nuns. They formed the backbone of this branch of Buddhism.

The Mayayana were encouraged to seek out through prayer a *bodhisattva* — a follower of Buddha who was able to reach Nirvana but delayed doing so in order to help lessen the suffering of others and guide them to their own enlightenment. (*Bodhi* means wise and *sattva* means being.) The *bodhisattvas* ruled over paradises that were like rest stops on the way to Nirvana. Praying to a *bodhisattva* was like praying to a saint of the Catholic Church.

Statues of a Buddha were placed in shrines throughout India. The figure, familiar to most people today, sat cross-legged in a meditating position. One palm was raised up, symbolizing his protection, and the other palm faced down, denoting a blessing.

Buddhism Arrives In China

By the 1st century AD, Buddhism of the Mahayana variety had entered China via the Silk Road. Eastern Han emperor Mingdi is said to have dreamed about a golden deity, who was later identified as Buddha.

The Five Virtues of Buddhism

1 — Not to harm any living thing
2 — Not to take what is not given
3 — Not to live in an over-excited way
4 — Not to say unkind things
5 — Not to take drugs or drink which will cloud the mind

ment of celibacy for monks ran contrary to the Chinese love of family and children. And the tonsure (the ritual shaving of the monk's head) violated the Confucian belief that altering the body from its natural state showed disrespect for the parents who had provided it. Finally, while the Buddhists considered all people equal, the Confucianists preferred their own system of social rankings.

Because of these conflicts, the Chinese came up with their own version of Buddhism. It emphasized inner peace and social harmony and described Nirvana as a place of eternal bliss where the souls of virtuous people mingled with divine spirits.

Buddhism in the North

During the Period of Division, many northern rulers adopted Buddhism as their official religion. In the 4th century a monk named Kumarajiva, who was fluent in Chinese and Sanskrit (the scholarly language of ancient India), came to the court in Chang'an to translate Buddhist texts that had been acquired over the years. He was assisted by more than a thousand Chinese monks. Together they completed the translation of 98 *sutras* (sacred texts) into their own language.

In 399 AD a monk named Faxian traveled from Chang-an to India to collect more Buddhist sutras. This was a difficult trek, especially for a man who was more

Intrigued, the emperor sent to India for copies of Buddhist *sutras* (religious scriptures). When these were translated into Chinese they led to an increased interest in Buddhism among his subjects.

By the end of the 2nd century, Buddhist communities had formed at Luoyang and other cities in northern China. There was some resistance among the Confucianists, however. The idea of looking forward to a state of nothingness ran counter to their interest in social harmony in the here and now. Of course, they also believed that the spirits of their ancestors lived in a celestial paradise, and that their own spirits would join them there some day. That concept was much more appealing than simply ceasing to exist. Furthermore, the require-

than 60 years old. Faxian decided to return by ship, but a storm carried his vessel hundreds of miles off course, and he spent nearly a year at sea. Fortunately, he managed to preserve the manuscripts, which he finally delivered to the court at Nanjing. His journal of his travels (*The Record of the Buddhist Countries*) would prove an invaluable source of information about ancient India. (Does this remind you of Zhang Qian of Western Han times? There are indeed many similarities.)

The greatest patrons of Buddhism in northern China during this period were the Tuoba. They sponsored several projects to carve huge Buddhist figures out of the faces of cliffs near the northern frontier. The first was begun in 366 AD near Dunhuang. The sandstone cliffs there rose above the muddy waters of the Dachuan river on the edge of the sandy wastes of the Gobi Desert.

For the next thousand years, monks and other workers filled hundreds of grottoes (caves) cut into the cliff face with statues of Buddha and wall paintings illustrating episodes from the life of Buddha and scenes from the sacred Buddhist texts. Today 492 of these elaborately decorated caves, known as the Caves of the Thousand Buddhas (*Qianfodong*), are open to visitors.

The following century, a similar project was begun in Yungang (near Datong, in Shanxi province). The Tuoba emperor commissioned a well-known Buddhist monk

Buddhism added a number of symbolic plants and creatures to the ancient Chinese culture. One of the best known is the lotus, a wild aquatic plant with large pink blossoms. The lotus grows through the muddy water of swamps, which, for the Buddhists, symbolized the mundane (everyday) world. It emerged through the muck clean and beautiful. This, as perhaps you've guessed, symbolized enlightenment. Many statues of the Buddha portray him seated in an open lotus flower.

named Tanyao to carve five huge statues of Buddha out of the cliff faces. He was later joined by hundreds of other monks. As in Dunhuang, this project was continued over many centuries.

Eventually, not five but over 100,000 sculptures of all sizes were chiseled in caves lining the steep river cliffs. The largest was 55 feet high, while the smallest was about half an inch. In one cave alone there were 10,000 figures of Buddha, as well as *bod-*

hisattvas and guardian creatures. A vast series of religious paintings were created over a period of nearly a thousand years. They would cover over 484,000 square feet on the walls of the cave temples.

When the Tuoba moved their capital to Luoyang, work began on a new cave complex in Longmen, which was not far from the city. Over 2,000 caves had been carved by nature out of the rock walls of a narrow canyon cut by the Yi River. Over the years, workmen carved out hundreds of niches into the caves and filled them with over 97,000 religious statues.

Luoyang became the center of Buddhism in eastern Asia. Temples and monasteries occupied a third of the city. One Tuoba ruler became so fascinated with the sutras that he abdicated the throne to devote himself to religious scholarship.

Buddhism in the South

Further south, Buddhist beliefs appealed to many of the educated Chinese who had already embraced Daoism. Many people found relief from the turbulent times in the peace and quiet of monastic life.

In time, it was not unusual to see groups of monks — with shaved heads and saffron robes — mingling with officials at the court at Nanjing and even advising the emperor. By the end of the Eastern Jin dynasty (420), there were 1,768 monasteries and 14,000 monks and nuns living in southern China.

Pagodas

In India, Buddhist *sutras* were usually housed in low, round brick buildings. These inspired the Chinese to build pagodas, which were originally round single-storied wooden buildings, whose sole purpose

Longmen means "Dragon Gate" in Chinese. An ancient legend described how at this site there was once a mountain, behind which lived a destructive dragon in a large body of water. Legendary emperor Yu got rid of the dragon by splitting the mountain open and giving it passage to the sea.

was to hold Buddhist writings. The first Chinese pagoda, constructed in Nanjing in the middle of the 3rd century, has not survived to our times.

Eventually, these low buildings evolved into tall towers on a square base. They actually looked like several one-story buildings stacked on top of one another, each with its own roof. The oldest surviving pagoda, built in 532 near Mount Song in Henan province, is 131 feet high. In later centuries, elegant pagodas would be built of stone and brick in the shape of octagons and hexagons.

The Later Dynasties in the South

For over a century, the Eastern Jin provided relative stability for the people living in southern China. The peaceful times came to an end in 420, when General Liu Yu usurped the throne and established a new dynasty, the Liu Song. Emperor Gong, the last Jin ruler, was a devout Buddhist. When Liu Yu ordered him to commit suicide by taking poison, Gong refused. Buddhists will not take a human life, including their own. So the guards smothered the emperor with a bedcover!

Four succeeding dynasties ruled during a period of 170 years following the fall of

The lion was not native to China, and perhaps this is why it came to be portrayed as a a unique beast (a cross between a lion and a dog) with a short, thick body, curly mane, bulging eyes, and a wide mouth. Buddhists considered the lion a defender of their religion, and for this reason stone lions squatting on their hind legs were often placed on either side of gates to temples and palaces. The creature was also called a *Fu* dog or *Fu* lion, *Fu* meaning Buddha in Chinese.

the Eastern Jin. Each dynasty was begun by a general who seized the throne in a bloody coup, and each ended in much the same way. The Liu Song dynasty lasted until 479,

The oldest surviving wooden building in China is the Buddhist temple of Nanchansi (built 782).

when it was replaced by the Southern Qi.

In 502 the Liang dynasty replaced the Southern Qi. It proved to be the most stable of the dynasties that followed the Eastern Jin, although it didn't last long. The Liang emperor took the name of Wudi. (There were, in fact, several Wudi's in ancient China.) He was a man of the people, who worked to reduce the political power of the wealthy nobles by encouraging men from all classes to seek government positions. He set an example by promoting his personal servant to a military position — in later years, the man became his most successful general. He founded five academies, and he required that all sons of nobles attend them to learn about the Confucian classics. Wudi also composed poetry and patronized the arts, drawing writers and painters to his court.

In his later years, Wudi became an ardent Buddhist. He banned meat and wine from the royal table (Buddhists are vegetarians), wrote commentaries on Buddhist texts, and held huge gatherings in which monks (and sometimes the emperor himself) lectured to groups of Liang citizens about the Buddhist scriptures. He honored the life of every living thing and forbade the use of animals for medicinal study or for sacrifices. For ancestral rites, he ordered that the sacrificial animals be replaced by pastry imitations. He even forbad the weaving of cloth with designs of men or animals,

since they might be cut when the material was used. According to official records, Wudi once had himself held hostage until the court raised a great sum of ransom money, which he then used to build Buddhist temples and monasteries. One of these was large enough to house 1,000 monks.

When Wudi died, several of his sons vied for power. None had inherited his gentle soul. Yuandi, who ruled for awhile, favored Daoism, although this didn't stop him from committing several acts of cruely against his rivals. He was convinced that his collection of Daoist texts had magical powers of protection. When Nanjing was attacked by a grandson of Wudi, he deliberately burned his library of over 200,000 books for failing him! The Liang were soon defeated by the last of the Southern Dynasties, the Chen.

Meanwhile, In Northern China...

In 515, the Tuoba ruler (of the Northern Wei dynasty) died. His widow, Empress Dowager Ling, seized power as regent for her young son. The empress was a remarkable athlete, who could outshoot any archer in the army. She was also a devout Buddhist. She ordered the construction of the Yongning Temple, a huge monastery in Luoyang. Its soaring bell tower could be seen from 30 miles away. Building the temple nearly depleted the treasury, and this created a public outcry (even among Buddhists).

Adding to the protest were the cries of Touba soldiers who felt their culture had become too Chinese. In 528 a general led a coup, which resulted in the empress and her son being drowned in the Yellow River. After six more years of unrest the Yongning Temple was destroyed and the Northern Wei dynasty of the Touba came to an end.

The north was split in two until 581, when Yang Jian, a general of combined Chinese and foreign ancestry founded yet another dynasty, the Sui (swee). This dynasty was the first in a long while to offer the hope of a truly united China.

(Take some time to digest and review what you've learned about the Age of Disunion before continuing on.)

The Sui Dynasty

A Bloodless Coup

After gaining control of the north, Yang Jian turned his attention to the south. He came up with a masterful scheme to absorb the southern territory without great bloodshed. It was simple. He circulated over 300,000 copies of a document denouncing crimes allegedly made by the Chen ruler. Claiming the man was unworthy of the Mandate of Heaven, the document urged the people to revolt against him. Everyone in the south began arguing about what to do, some eager to oust the Chen leader and others preferring to reserve judgment. The government itself was in turmoil. This is when Yang Jian quietly sent down his troops. They were able to defeat the Chen without meeting any strong resistance. China was reunited at last.

Wendi's Regime

Yang Jian is known to us as Wendi. (Yes, another Wendi. This name was almost as popular as Wudi among Chinese emperors.) He proved to be a wise and fair-minded ruler. Although he sacked Nanjing, he treated the Chen people leniently. He realized that he was an outsider in Chinese society (remember, the northern kingdoms were ruled by foreigners) and needed to widen his range of support. He hoped to win the Chinese to his side by adopting

Wendi had great respect for the intelligence of his first wife, the empress, and he received a good deal of advice from her. So he honored her demand that he have no concubines. Unfortunately, he fell in love with another woman in later life. When the empress heard about this, she had the girl murdered! The grieving emperor allegedly lamented, as he rode through the mountains, "I may be honored as the Son of Heaven, but I have no freedom."

many features of the Han government. But while he appointed many Chinese as lower-ranked officials, he placed his relatives and close allies in the top positions. To ensure internal peace, he disbanded the private armies that had flourished during the earlier centuries of disunity and organized an imperial army under strict central control.

Wendi created a new code of law that was fair and equitable. He distributed large tracts of land to the peasants, whom he required to pay three taxes: a land tax payable in grain, a cloth tax payable in silk, and a labor tax requiring 20 days of labor per year from adult males. Wendi was not without his faults. He often flew into violent rages, once beating an official to death!

Chang'an was to be the Sui capital, and Wendi ordered the construction of many new buildings there, including a large palace. The palace had a pavilion for several hundred guests that could be rotated by a mechanism underneath. Startled visitors swore they were being moved about by one of the gods! The emperor couldn't have been more delighted with this awesome "special effect."

Wendi had been born and raised in a Buddhist temple, so, of course, he was a strong supporter of Buddhism. He ordered 4,000 new Buddhist temples built throughout his empire. Over 100,000 new images of the Buddha were made to fill them, while older ones that had been broken were restored.

The Civil Service Exams

As a Buddhist, Wendi felt little kinship with the Confucian scholars. He once sneered indignantly at one who disagreed with him, shouting out "You bookworm!" However, he realized that Confucian ideals could strengthen Chinese society as well as the government itself, and so he reinstituted the civil service examinations. As before, the exams tested candidates in "the classics," as well as Chinese history up to their own times. They also had to write essays on moral principles and solve practical problems that might arise in the running of a government.

Yangdi's Expensive Projects

In 604 Wendi died. He was succeeded by his second son, who ruled as Yangdi. Like his father, Yangdi combined his devout Buddhism with a support for Confucian studies.

Yangdi rebuilt Luoyang as a second capital, dipping deeply into the treasury to make the city truly grand. Two million workers labored to create magnificent palaces, artificial lakes, and a pleasure park covering 60 square miles. (When the emperor visited the city in winter, the bare branches were decked with silk flowers and leaves to give the appearance of warmer times.)

Yangdi's major project was the building of a vast canal system. This project had, in fact, been begun by Wendi, but Yangdi carried it out to amazing ends. Rivers and streams were widened and connected to an extensive thoroughfare, the Grand Canal, that linked the Yellow River and other river systems of the north with the Huai, the Yangzi, and the smaller rivers to the south. The network of canals covered nearly 1200 miles.

This project was the most dramatic improvement in connecting parts of the empire since the First Emperor's highway system and his Magic Transport Canal. But it was also very expensive in terms of funds and labor. All available men (commoners) between the ages of 15 and 50 worked on it, and families living near the site had to send an old man, a woman, and a child to distribute food to the labor force.

When the project was completed, Yangdi commissioned a fleet of ships shaped like dragons to carry his entire court down the Grand Canal. His entourage of 80,000 people included the imperial family, ministers and court officials, priests and ambassadors, followed by servants and attendants. The emperor's boat had four decks with private apartments, a throne room, and 120 exquisitely decorated rooms for all his concubines. Gangs of men ran along paths beside the canals pulling the boats of the Dragon Fleet with ropes of green silk. As they progressed, the passengers were entertained by the imperial musicians. It was a magnificent — and costly — production.

The Grand Canal, the world's longest artificially created waterway, is still in use today.

Yangdi Loses His Support

Yangdi's foreign policies were also big-budget items. He sent troops to take over and patrol oasis cities along the Silk Road. He sent other forces to North Vietnam, and he opened diplomatic relations with Japan. He launched several campaigns against Koguryo, a kingdom in Korea. All were unsuccessful, with crippling losses of life and money.

Yangdi was so preoccupied with his foreign ventures that he didn't notice the growing unrest at home. Masses of Chinese were protesting his expensive projects and seemingly unending demands for manpower. (This was a common complaint in ancient China, wasn't it?) When the Yellow River flooded the countryside, adding to the misery of the local people, the rebellions escalated.

A story was told that when Yangdi heard the king of Koguryo refused to pay homage to him, he had the king's ambassador in China killed, cooked, and served to his troops for dinner!

The Fall of the Sui

While all these things were happening, a fortuneteller told Yangdi that he would soon be overthrown by a man named Li. But Li was one of the most common names in China. Which Li could it be? According to legend, the emperor had every official in the capital with that name executed. But in 617 a provincial governor named Li Yuan captured Chang'an. Yangdi abdicated and fled south to Jiangdu, where he spent most of his time meditating. One of his bodyguards later killed him and his son.

The emperor's grandson, Gongdi, was then placed on the throne, with Li Yuan serving as regent. The following year, Li Yuan captured Luoyang. He then disposed of Gongdi.

The Sui dynasty had not lasted very long. However, it had served an important function. China was again united and a well-organized government had been set in motion. In this way, it can be compared with the Qin dynasty of Shi Huangdi.

Li Yuan declared himself the founder of the Tang (tong) Dynasty, which he named after his fiefdom in modern Shanxi province. China was entering a fabulous new age, one that would surpass in many ways the shining era of the Han.

REVIEW QUESTIONS

1. What were the major time periods of the Age of Division?
2. What was *The Romance of the Three Kingdoms*?
3. Who were the Seven Sages of the Bamboo Grove?
4. What caused the fall of the Western Jin?
5. Into what major parts was China divided during the Period of Disunion?
6. How did the move south affect the Chinese scholars?
7. What were the Four Noble Truths?
8. What were the two branches of Buddhism, and how did they differ?
9. What was a *bodhisattva*?
10. Who was Faxian?
11. Describe the statues in Dunhuang.
12. What is a pagoda?
13. What good things did Wendi do for China?
14. Why was Yangdi so unpopular with his subjects?
15. What new dynasty did Li Yuan found?

PROJECTS

1. The Age of Division has been likened to the Dark Ages in Europe. Find out about the Dark Ages. What similarities do you see between that period and China's Age of Division? Make a chart to indicate similarities and differences between these two time periods.

2. Zhuge Liang, minister of Liu Bei, has been called the Chinese Machiavelli. Find out who Machiavelli was. Then find out more about Zhuge Liang. Make a Venn Diagram comparing these two men.

3. See if your library has a copy of *The Romance of the Three Kingdoms*. Read several chapters. Then write a skit based on the episodes your read about. Act out the skit for your classmates.

4. Fu Jian was a Chinese-educated Tibetan general who, in 357, began a rule of the central provinces in the north. By 376 he ruled all of northern China and controlled the western trade routes. He dreamed of controlling all of China. In 383 he led his army south. Find out what happened during this historical campaign. Share your findings with your classmates.

5. The lotus was an important Buddhist symbol. It was also a symbol in ancient Egypt. Find out the meaning of the lotus in ancient Egyptian art and religion. Then learn more about the use of the lotus in Buddhist art. Write a short report about the symbolism of this flower in ancient cultures.

6. Write a short play about the life of Buddha.

7. Draw a picture of a Buddha, or make one out of clay.

8. Make a Venn Diagram comparing Shi Huangdi and Wendi.

9. *Shih tzu* means lion in Chinese. This is also the name of the breed of a toy dog popular in the United States. Find out what the little long-haired shih tzu dog (an import from Tibet) has in common with the stone lions (also called *fu* dogs) that guarded the tombs of ancient Chinese emperors. Make a poster illustrating your discoveries.

10. Find out more about meditation. Then lead your classmates in a group meditation experience. Serve tea afterwards, if you like, to help everyone "wake up."

Happenings Elsewhere during the Age of Division (220 - 589)

Sassanian empire established in Persia (226)

Classical Period of Mayan Civilization, Central America (c 250 - 850)

Reign of Constantine of Rome (312 - 337)

Angles, Saxons, and Jutes invade England (449)

Fall of the last Western Roman Emperor (476)

Reign of Clovis, King of the Franks (481 - 511)

Beginning of Mississippian culture in North America (c500)

Saint Benedict founds monastery at Monte Cassino, Italy (529)

Gupta Empire collapses in India (535)

Life of Prophet Mohammed, founder of Islam(570 – 632)

The *shou*, a symbol of good health and long life

CHAPTER 8

THE TANG DYNASTY

CHINA'S GOLDEN AGE
(618— 906)

The Tang dynasty marks the beginning of a thousand-year period during which China was one of the wealthiest and most powerful countries in the world. The Tang built upon traditions dating from the Han dynasty, adding new perspectives and innovations that remain a part of Chinese culture today. For this reason, historians consider the Tang dynasty a turning point between ancient and modern times. And because of the many extraordinary works of poetry and art that were produced, this period is also known as China's Golden Age.

Peace Returns to China

The country was still badly torn apart by rebel factions when Li Yuan founded his new dynasty. With the help of his second son, Li Shimin (Lee Shur meen), he put down the rebellions and restored peace to China. He made Chang'an his capital. As first emperor of the Tang, Li Yuan became known as Gaozu.

One of the first things he did once peace was restored was to grant a pardon to the Sui imperial family and their followers, and he even appointed former Sui officials to his government. As earlier rulers had already discovered, this strategy helped to heal the wounds of civil war. Gaozu also revised the code of laws and promoted the civil service examination system. He took away portions of the land from the wealthy families and rented them to the peasants. This led to a greater production of food and happier peasants. It also cut the power of the nobles.

Like the Han, the Tang government had three top ministries. These were the Secretariat, the Chancellery, and the Department of State Affairs. The Secretariat

Highlights of This Chapter

TheTang Bureaucracy
The Reign of Taizong
Empress Wu
The Brilliant Emperor
The Great Poets
Landscape Painting
Ceramics
The Printing of Books
The Invention of Gunpowder

was responsible for drafting official documents and imperial edicts. The Chancellery examined and approved documents prepared by the Secretariat. (Policies that were accepted were passed on to the emperor for his final approval.) The Department of State Affairs put new policies into effect. It ran the courts and enforced the laws. Six lesser ministries dealt with taxation, military affairs, public construction projects, education, waterways, and the imperial stables.

The country was now divided into prefectures and districts, governed by lower level officials. The emperor kept track of the activities of officials serving in distant provinces by sending commissioners to check up on them.

Gaozu was not a Buddhist, and he did not support the religion. He issued an official edict defining Daoism and Confucianism as the two pillars of Chinese culture. He even claimed to be descended from Laozi, and he built an ancestral temple at the site where Laozi was supposedly born. He also built a temple for the worship of Confucius (now considered a god) at Chang'an.

Grand Ancestor Tang

Gaozu's reign came to an abrupt end when his son, Li Shimin, grabbed power for himself. Looking back, such a move was somewhat predictable. As a teenager of 16, Li Shimin had helped persuade his father to rise against the Sui, and once the Tang dynasty was founded, he had fought at his side to restore peace. For these reasons, he felt that he deserved to be next in line to become emperor. But he was a second son, and his older brother was officially recognized as the heir.

Both brothers had their supporters, and the court became the scene of many arguments about who should succeed Gaozu. In 626 Li Shimin led a coup that resulted in the death of his older brother, and, for good measure, his younger brother was killed as well. But being next in line to the throne was no longer enough. He forced his father into retirement and declared himself emperor.

Li Shimin took the name of Tang Taizong (tong tai tsung, "Grand Ancestor Tang"). Grand Ancestor? Wouldn't that be Gaozu? Not according to his son, who claimed that *he* had masterminded the overthrow of the Sui and brought the Tang dynasty into being. Taizong later edited the official histories to support this claim. (Most historians believe that while Li Shimin had fought and worked beside his father, Gaozu was clearly in charge.)

Despite the violent means by which he acquired power and the questionable merit of his claims as founder of the new dynasty, Taizong proved to be one of the truly great emperors of ancient China.

A Scholar at the Helm

Taizong's talents went beyond military leadership. He had been well educated in the Confucian classics, and he was a keen scholar. His intellectual interests were reflected in his government. He created the Bureau of Historiography, which kept historical records. (Their records included, of course, the emperor's "rewriting" of history to cast himself as the Tang founder.) He also established the Academy of Sages, a group of authors who composed literary works for the court, and the Bureau for the Progress of Literature, which prepared the emperor's speeches.

To further strengthen his credentials, Taizong organized the leading families of northeastern China into four categories, then ranked them. Of course, the Li clan was listed at the top! He also created a system of state academies, reserving one for the children of the imperial family and those of the highest officials.

Taizong was very mindful of the turmoil that had been caused by the extravagant spending and labor demands of Yangzi, and, at least during the early part of his reign, he limited the number and scope of public works projects. However, he put endless hours into his own official paperwork — so many, in fact, that his ministers had to work in shifts to keep up with him, and they pasted documents he had not read during the day on his bedroom walls to read just before he went to sleep. In this respect, he was a lot like Shi Huangdi, wasn't he?

The Empire Expands

Do you remember how huge the empire became under the Western Han? During the Age of Division, much of this land was lost, but you've seen how Sui emperor Yangdi won back some of the western territory. Taizong made the expansion of his realm a major goal.

From the start, he relied upon a combination of military force and skillful diplomacy (and cunning!). When the Eastern Turks, a confederation of tribesmen, invaded China and came within 75 miles of Chang'an, he sent out a secret force of spies, who infiltrated the enemy camps. He soon learned that the Turks had split into two warring factions. So he openly threw his support behind one side. Once this faction defeated the other, he sent envoys to convince the tribesmen to settle their differences. Peace was restored among the Eastern Turks, who now resettled *outside* the Chinese borders as Taizong's allies. He

Mounted soldiers wore various styles of metal breastplates. They were elaborately decorated and colored. Often they had bright metal discs on the breast straps to reflect the light to dazzle or frighten the enemy.

later used a similar tactic with the Western Turks.

Imperial troops gradually regained control of the trading centers that had sprung up along the Silk Road as far as present-day Kirghizstan. By renewing contact with the merchants of western Asia, Taizong promoted a trade network that would make China richer than it had ever been. He also established diplomatic relations with Byzantium (in modern Turkey) and the Sassanian Empire in Iran. Before long, ambassadors from many distant countries were mingling with foreign merchants and Chinese officials in Chang'an.

Tibet was a mountainous kingdom southwest of China. Taizong arranged a peace treaty with its powerful king and sent a Tang princess in marriage to seal the deal. Tibet became a powerful ally, an important asset for rulers of future dynasties. The emperor also extended his southern boundaries into present-day Vietnam.

His efforts to conquer the kingdom of Koguryo were less successful. Nonetheless, under Taizong's reign China controlled as much territory as it had in Han times.

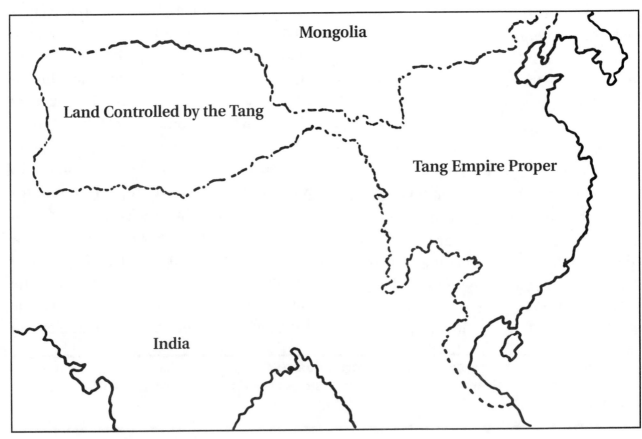

A Splendid Capital

During the Tang dynasty Chang'an became the largest and most cosmopolitan capital in the world, with a population of more than one million. Much of the city had been destroyed in the fighting that ended the Western Han dynasty. Taizong rebuilt and expanded it to cover nearly 30 square miles. The surrounding walls were three stories high, with even higher gatehouses. A grand avenue nearly 500 feet wide led from the southern gate to the imperial palace, which lay in the heart of the city, then continued on to the northern gate. It cut the rest of Chang'an in two — the eastern and western sections.

The city was further divided into 108 rectangular wards, each surrounded by a wall that was entered by four gates. (A ward was like a small city within a large one.) The wards in the western section were inhabited by merchants, workers, and craftsmen. Every night large drums were beaten to signal the closing of the ward gates. No one was allowed on the streets after dark except the armed soldiers who patrolled them. Bells in the temples and watchtowers were struck at daybreak to mark the reopening of the gates.

The eastern section of Chang'an was called "the Imperial City." It was made up of boulevards lined with the elegant estates of the wealthy officials. Each estate was a separate ward, surrounded by a wall with gatehouses and watchtowers. In this way, the wealthy people lived much as they did in Chang'an during the Western Han dynasty.

North of the palace were beautiful parks, where bamboo leaves rustled in the wind, lotus flowers floated on artificial ponds, and wisteria with tumbling blue flowers wound around open "summer houses."

There were two large markets, east and west. The eastern market was fairly small and served the needs of the wealthy households. The western market was huge. It drew thousands of merchants from such faraway places as Syria, Persia, and India. Visitors to this bustling marketplace were often entertained by strolling players, street acrobats, and storytellers.

Fashions of Dress

Taizong's court was the heart of fashion for the privileged elite. Courtiers and their wives (yes, wives were at last allowed to attend the court activities) wore flowing

---

The Tang required all "foreign" states that formed part of the empire or dealt with the emperor to send gifts (pay tribute) to the court as a way of demonstrating their acceptance of China's superiority. In addition to exotic treasures, the tribute included dancing girls from Persia, musicians from Vietnam, and acrobats from Korea.

and arranged in a topknot, held in place by delicately carved hairpins and combs. She wore thick make-up — layers of carefully applied face powder and rouge. It was considered fashionable to have a pale face (with rosy cheeks), as opposed to the tanned skin of a peasant who labored in the sun. Most women used so much powder that their faces were a ghostly white. Clothing, on the other hand, was most colorful.

Colors always had symbolic meanings in ancient China. Yellow, of course, was

silk garments that fell to their feet. The sleeves of the men's robes were so wide they were often weighted down so they would hang without flapping. The men wore elaborate headgear that reflected their position and status. Many hats were made from lacquered cloth or even leather. One was shaped like a water chestnut!

A noble woman wore a long skirt and jacket, topped by a short-sleeved upper garment. Her shoes were made of silk brocade. (Brocade is silk cloth that has patterns woven into it.) Her long hair was gathered

A typical peasant family shared a small one-room house of mud-bricks. In some regions, the sound of a drum called the farmers together and then beat out a work rhythm. (The drum could be heard from sunrise to sunset.)

the imperial color, and only the emperor and his sons could wear a yellow silk robe. The emperor's grandsons wore purple, the color of promise or potential. Red was a lucky color, associated with the sun, happiness, and *yang*. It also symbolized virtue and truth. At a wedding the bride wore a red robe, while the groom wore green. White was the color of mourning, and no one could wear a white robe while his parents were alive. Black was associated with guilt, although, of course, in Qin times it had a more positive meaning. (Black, remember, was associated with water in the table of the Five Elements.)

While the members of the upper classes wore bright colors, the common people were forbidden to do so. In 674 AD the government passed strict laws to stop people from hiding "forbidden" colors underneath their outer garments. (This was actually directed at the merchants, since only they could easily afford to wear brightly colored silk.)

Peasants wore a long, shirt-like garment, made of undyed hemp fiber, over loose trousers that ended at mid-calf. These outfits, which resembled modern pajamas, were loose fitting and allowed plenty of movement in the fields. (The shortened trousers were ideal for working barefoot in the rice paddies.) Cotton was not introduced into China until around the 6th century, when it replaced hemp as the most popular cloth among the lower classes. A peasants' sandals were made of rushes or straw. In the south, broad-brimmed, cone-shaped hats were worn to protect the workers' faces from the hot sun and heavy rain.

The Travels of Xuan Zang

Although Taizong had little interest in Buddhism, he did hold an important audience with a Buddhist monk just the year before he died. This man, Xuan Zang, had just returned from India, and he had many an exciting tale to tell.

The monk had set out from Chang'an in 629 on a quest for answers to many questions that he could not find in the Chinese translations of the Buddhist texts. These texts had been copied and recopied so many times since they were first translated that they had become inaccurate and incomplete. (A few mistakes were inevitable in copying a long book, and once they were made they were repeated in all future copies.)

He traveled more than 1,500 miles, passing through present-day Ganzu province, then to the north of the Gobi Desert, eventually descending to India through present-day Afghanistan. He stayed for a while in Kashmir, a great center of scholarship, then moved on to Mathura and finally to Nalanda, a long established Buddhist university in eastern India.

Xuan Zang spent many years in

India, learning Sanskrit, debating with religious scholars, and collecting Buddhist *sutras*. He also came in contact with some of the greatest rulers of the day, including the famous playwright-king, Harsha. At last, after accumulating 657 manuscripts, he set out on his return to China.

He arrived in 645, after an absence of 16 years. He was greeted by great crowds of monks and government officials. This is when Taizong received him. The emperor was so impressed by the texts he had brought that he provided the monk with all the assistance he needed to translate them into Chinese. He also gave him a generous a salary — for life. (Taizong would even convert to Buddhism, just before he died.)

So Xuan Zang gladly settled down to his new task. More than a fifth of the huge body of surviving Buddhist materials in Chinese that exist today were translated by this industrious monk. In 652 the Big Wild Goose Pagoda was built to house the manuscripts he had gathered and translated.

Xuan Zang's lively description of his travels (*Record of the Western Realms*) remains an invaluable source of information about the kingdoms he visited. (See the box below.)

Planning for the Future

Toward the end of his life, Taizong worried about who would succeed him as emperor. His heir, Li Cheng Qian (the eldest of his 14 sons), was considered an eccentric. Having become obsessed with his "barbarian" ancestry, the prince wore Turkish clothes, spoke only the Turkish language, and lived in a felt tent — stealing sheep and cooking them in nomad fashion over a camp fire. Outraged by this behavior, many officials threw their support behind a younger son, Li Tai. The growing conflict over who should inherit the throne was

Xuan Zang's journey also provided the inspiration for the 16th century novel by Wu Cheng'en, *Record of a Journey to the West*. It is one of the most widely read books in Chinese literature, combining elements of Daoism, Buddhism, and ancient folklore. The hero is not Xuan Zang, but rather a magical character known as Monkey. He gets into all kinds of mischief before he even meets Xuan Zang. (Among other things, he eats the magic peaches of the Queen of the West!) Together, Monkey and Xuan Zang set out for India. They are soon joined by two other humorous characters — Pigsy (who eats too much) and Sandy (who is always getting confused). The little band has extraordinary adventures on the way to India, encountering a bizarre cast of demons, spirits, gods, and *bodhisattvas*.

Stories from the book are featured in modern cartons and TV ads in China, and every Chinese child knows all about Monkey, Pigsy, and Sandy — and the pilgrim monk — just as American children are familiar with the characters of Walt Disney.

resolved when the two sons attempted plots against each other *and* against the emperor. In 643, Taizong ousted them both and chose his ninth son, Li Zhi, as his heir.

With that matter taken care of, the emperor could face his final days with a lighter heart. Years earlier, construction had begun on his tomb. A tunnel had been cut into the side of a huge mountain, and within it a mortuary palace to house his coffin was built, as well as a replica of Chang'an. The spirit road leading to the tomb entrance was lined with 68 stone statues, averaging 13 feet in height. It was an impressive final resting-place.

The Empress Wu

Taizong died in 649, and 20-year-old Li Zhi took the throne. He ruled as Gaozong. Unfortunately, the young man suffered from frequent attacks of dizziness, which made it difficult for him to function normally. In addition to his fragile health, he had a weak character and was easily manipulated by other people. And he had no talent at all for running an empire. His reign did not look at all promising. One wonders why Taizong selected him among his other eligible sons.

It wasn't long before Gaozong enraged the government officials by replacing his legal wife with one of his concubines, Wu Zhao. Wu was an incredibly ambitious woman, and the emperor was like putty in her hands. Her rise to power was steeped in blood. She suffocated her own newborn daughter and then accused Gaozong's wife, Wang, of the crime. Wang was found guilty and dethroned. (According to some records, Wu Zhao saw to it that the arms and legs of the ex-empress, as well as those of the emperor's favorite concubine Xiao, were amputated. Then she had what remained of them thrown into a wine vat!)

Now Wu Zhao set her sights on grabbing the reins of power. First, she had her son declared heir. Then, using guile and deceit, she wormed her way into the center of power. Before long, she was actually acting in the emperor's name. When Gaozong was left half-blind and paralyzed by a stroke in 660, his wife became the effective ruler of China. Even when he died and was succeeded by his son, Wu Zhao was running the show. She eliminated anyone who stood in her way. (Doesn't she remind you of Empress Lu of the Western Han?)

Wu was a Buddhist, perhaps because the Buddhists believed that women were as important as men. (The most popular *bodhisattva* in China, Guanyin, was portrayed as a woman.) Wu founded numerous

One of history's earliest feminists, Wu Zhao founded a scholarly institute to compile a "Collection of Biographies of Famous Women."

Buddhist monasteries. Many of these were dedicated to an ancient text (conveniently "discovered" by one of her Buddhist supporters), which predicted that a woman would be born of such merit that she would become the Maitreya, the Future Buddha. (The text was fake, of course, and had been created to her own specifications!) In 673 Wu commissioned the carving and placement of a monumental statue of the Maitreya at Longmen. The statue's features and expressions, which vary according to angle of viewing, closely resemble those of the infamous concubine.

Despite great opposition by the court officials, Wu Zhao decided to make Luoyang a second Tang capital. For a few years, she moved her court seasonally from one capital city to the other, at great expense and inconvenience. Finally, she made Luoyang the single capital in 683, probably because most of the Tang nobility lived in the original capital, Chang'an. (She had few supporters among them.) To reaffirm her own royal status, she built an imperial temple for her ancestors at Luoyang. This sparked a revolt among the nobles, who had had enough of Wu's pretensions. She put down the revolt in three months, and because she now worried about future uprisings, she created a secret police force. It's a good thing she did, too, because the Tang princes joined together in another rebellion in 688. Her police nipped that revolt in the bud and eliminated not only the princes but nearly all members of the imperial family. She was clearly not a woman to tangle with!

In 689 Wu deposed the young emperor and founded a new dynasty (the Zhou), taking for herself the name of Empress Wu Zetian. She was the only woman in Chinese history to rule the empire in her own name. (Other women ruled ancient China from "behind the throne," but Wu was the only female monarch.) Do you remember the story of the Nine Caldrons? (See page 75.) Wu ordered a set of caldrons to be cast as a means of bolstering her dubious claim to the throne. Of course, she told everyone that these were the original caldrons dating from the times of Emperor Yu of the Xia!

Empress Wu took the phoenix as her symbol. The phoenix was a mythical bird that represented *yin*, and so it was associated with women. (The original phoenix was, of course, one of the four special animals that helped Pangu create the world.) Like the dragon, the Chinese phoenix had the attributes of many beasts — it had the head of a pheasant, the beak of a parrot, the body

---

Many Buddhist statues were huge. During the reign of Taizong a monk started sculpting the Da-fu (dah foo) or "Big Buddha" out of a cliff above a river in Sichuan. It stood 156 feet high. The ears were longer than a two-story house is high. This giant sculpture took 90 years to finish.

of a duck, the wings of a roc (another myth-ical bird), the feathers of a peacock, and the legs of a crane. The phoenix would become the symbol of all future empresses.

Empress Wu proved to be a very capable ruler. She was intelligent, politically savvy, and an excellent judge of men. For 20 years, she continued the policies of her hus-band and his father, Taizong. She main-tained peace at home (no one was about to challenge her authority!) and conducted an active policy of expansion, carrying Chinese power to its furthest point ever. (During her reign China was the largest empire in the world.)

In 697, the aging empress became infatuated with two brothers (the Zhangs), who paraded around her court in strange costumes and looked down their noses at her ministers. This went on for several years, until, in 705, a group of senior offi-cials arranged a plot. The Zhang brothers were killed and the empress (who was now in her eighties) was forced to abdicate. She died (of natural causes) later that year.

Empress Wu was one of the most controversial women in Chinese history. But despite her ruthlessness and self-absorption, she provided strong leadership and brought peace and prosperity to her people. She also proved that a woman could efficiently wield power in a man's world.

The phoenix was usually depicted in paintings and embroideries with the dragon (symbol of the emperor). In later times, dragon and phoenix came to stand for man and wife. Engagement cer-tificates would be called "dragon-phoenix papers," and wedding cakes would be known as "dragon-phoenix cakes."

The "Brilliant Emperor"

In 712 Xuanzong (shoo an sahng, "Profound Ancestor"), the most popular of all Chinese emperors, came to the throne. His reign marked the high point of Tang art and culture. Because of his achievements, he is also known as *Ming Huang* (ming who-ahng, "Brilliant Emperor").

Xuanzong's childhood had been overshadowed by his grandmother, Wu Zetian. She had his mother murdered and kept his father's family virtual prisoners in the palace! In spite of his difficult beginnings, or perhaps because of them, he would rule with a keen sense of justice and fair play. He adhered to the Confucian ideal that a ruler should do all he can to benefit his people.

A Return to Chang'an

Xuanzong made Chang'an the capital once again. It was one of the most densely populated cities in the world, with over a million people living within its walls and another million in the surrounding towns. (London at this time was just a market town of a few thousand people.)

Like most rulers of ancient China, Xuanzong worried about the possible threat of the tribesmen living just beyond the northern borders. He divided the frontier into nine sectors, placing each sector under the command of a military governor, who had a large force of professional soldiers to deal with any threats of invasion.

China's most important trading seaport was Guangzhou (modern Canton). During Xuanzong's reign, it became a huge metropolis of traders and merchants.

A New Bridge

You've already learned about the network of canals and rivers that connected the Yellow River with the Yangzi. (Remember Yangdi's Grand Canal?) But until 722, the main route from the north to the central plains and south depended on a pontoon bridge over the Yellow River built during the Western Jin dynasty. Trade and commerce were interrupted every year when the bridge was washed away in the spring floods.

Xuanzong ordered the construction of a permanent bridge. It was held in place by iron chains attached to four iron anchors on each riverbank. The anchors, which were molded in the form of oxen, were ten feet long and five feet high. Each ox stood atop a foundation that went 13 feet into the ground and weighed 70 tons, which was certainly sufficient to hold the bridge in place. This major project used one-third of China's total annual production of iron.

Chinese Cuisine

The wealthy officials and courtiers of these prosperous times often entertained one another at elaborate banquets. Many new types of food were introduced via the Silk Road or arrived as tribute from exotic places. Among these were dates, sugared

The Chinese were building suspension bridges as early as 1 AD using rope and bamboo. In 580 a bridge suspended from iron chains crossed the Yangzi River.

ginger, sea horses, melons, persimmons, and dried oysters.

Wine was served in great quantities at the banquets. It was acceptable to drink a lot of wine, because the alcohol relaxed a person and brought him or her closer to the spirits of the universe. (Consuming large quantities of alcohol was an old tradition. Do you remember how the noblemen of the Western Zhou dynasty were known to drink huge amounts of rice wine from their beautiful bronze goblets?)

Even ordinary people ate quite well during the Tang dynasty. Food was divided into two categories: grains (*fan*) and "vegetables" (*cai*). Grains were basically rice in the south and noodles or dumplings made from wheat in the north. The vegetable category actually included any food that wasn't a grain, including fish, fowl, and meat. Meat was rarely consumed, but when it was, pork or duck were the likely choices. Beef was not eaten, since oxen were considered valuable work animals. The most commonly eaten "true" vegetable was cabbage. Except during festivals, the grain, not the vegetables, was considered the main ingredient of most meals.

The dishes were seasoned with salt, plum and soy sauces, garlic, ginger, or even cinnamon. Honey was a favorite sweetener. Efforts were made to mix the five flavors — bitter, salty, sour, hot, and sweet — in the dishes of a single meal. Certain regions of China had specialties. Sichuan dishes were often livened up with hot chile peppers, while Yangzi dishes frequently included mushrooms and bamboo shoots.

Because wood and other fuel were scarce, food was cut into small pieces and cooked quickly on high heat in frying pans or in steamers. (Modern chefs use the same techniques because food cooked in this way is so healthy!) And because the food was served in manageable sizes, it was easily eaten with chopsticks. The Chinese never had the need for table knives and forks!

Each person was served his or her own bowl of *fan*, and the *cai* dishes were served in the center of the table in large bowls for all diners to share. Everyone helped himself to the vegetables using his chopsticks. For this reason, it was considered extremely rude to let your lips touch the tips of your chopsticks.

Tea (*cha*) became popular during the Tang Dynasty. It was not served with meals, but after the food was eaten. The Chinese

---

Today there are more than 250 varieties of Chinese tea. Their flavors differ according to where they were grown, the time of day and season the leaves were picked, and the methods of processing and brewing them. They are sold as loose tea leaves or compressed into cakes or bricks. Flowers (rosebuds and jasmin), ginger, and tangerine peel are sometimes added to the tea for special flavor.

believed the tea cleared the mind and aided digestion.

This beverage had been introduced during the Han dynasty by Buddhist monks, who drank it to stay awake during their long meditations. (Tea has caffeine, which is a stimulant.) *The Book of Tea*, written by Lu Yu in 760, described the cultivation and serving of tea. The tea leaves were picked from the tea shrub that grew in the southern Sichuan basin. They were laid out in the sun, rolled by hand, and then dried over charcoal fires. The tea was brewed by putting tea leaves in a heated clay teapot, heating fresh water to the boiling point, pouring the water over the leaves, and letting the tea sit (steep) for about five minutes.

From Cushions to Chairs

Another innovation introduced into China via the Silk Road was wooden furniture. In earlier times, the Chinese sat cross-legged on mats or cushions when they ate, socialized, or simply wanted to relax in their homes. By the 7th century, more substantial pieces of furniture were being imported from Persia, and furniture-making soon became an important Chinese industry. Without the benefit of nails, skilled craftsmen assembled elaborately carved tables and chairs. The most elegant of these, which ended up in the emperor's palace or the homes of the wealthiest officials, were made of rosewood and inlaid with ivory or mother-of-pearl.

There was even a hierarchy of chairs! High-ranking officials sat on armchairs with round or square backs. Those of military officials were covered with animal skins (preferably tiger, most ferocious of Chinese beasts), while others were decorated with silk cloth. Lower ranking men sat on chairs without arms. Ordinary people sat on stools. Portable folding chairs were used by officials when they were traveling. A "drunken lord's chair" was a lounge chair with a movable headrest and an extension at the end that could be pulled out to rest the feet.

Dining room furniture was placed against the walls when not in use in order to create as much open space as possible. (The Chinese disliked clutter, which interrupted the free flow of *qi*.) Decorative screens, which were used to separate areas and provide privacy, were also folded up and put away when not in use.

A Brilliant Court

Xuanzong took great pleasure in reading and composing poetry, and he found it fascinating to ponder the ideas expressed in both Buddhist and Daoist texts. He also enjoyed listening to music and watching dance performances. Given his intellectual and artistic interests, it is no surprise that he surrounded himself with people talented in these areas. He created the most brilliant court in Chinese history, drawing gifted men from all parts of China. (No wonder he's known as the Brilliant Emperor!)

Early in his reign, Xuanzong founded the Hanlin Academy, an organization of scholars whose function was to write diplomatic letters and literary compositions — particularly poetry — for the imperial court. (Hanlin means "Forest of Writing Brushes," a reference to the brushes used for calligraphy.) The Hanlin Academy would endure for many dynasties to come.

The Art of Poetry

The ability to compose poetry was so highly valued during the Tang era that it was a requirement on the civil service examinations. People often sent poems to one another in place of letters, and light-hearted poetry contests continued to be a popular form of entertainment at banquets and dinner parties.

The Chinese language lends itself to poetic interpretation. Because a character can be translated many different ways, it is up to the reader to determine what meaning fits best. (See page 108.) This can make the translation of a Chinese written passage a challenging task, particularly for someone who is not a native speaker. But this very richness of language has enabled Chinese poets to create wonderfully evocative verses. Since each word in a poem offers a variety of images, the reader is left to respond in a very personal way. A poem is thus very much like a painting — it creates a mood but speaks to different people in different ways.

The poems written during the reign of Xuanzong are considered among the richest in Chinese literature. Many express the beauty of a natural scene or the sorrow of missing someone. Others are social commentaries — witty descriptions of particular people, or bitter reflections on the contrast between the rich and poor. You've already discovered how the ancient Chinese enjoyed using symbols, like the dragon, the phoenix, and the peach. Such symbols abound in Chinese poetry. For example, a rose represents the fragility of human life, an evergreen tree suggests steadfastness, a peony means luxury, a bamboo represents flexibility, and a butterfly implies joy and

The Pear Garden (*Liyuan*) was Xuanzong's imperial academy of dance and music. He personally oversaw the training and rehearsals of hundreds of dancers and musicians. The Brilliant Emperor also arranged court music — in the "sitting mode" (chamber music, played by 3 to 12 musicians) and the "standing mode" (orchestra music played in the open air by 60 to 180 musicians).

longevity. (Why longevity? Because the Chinese word for butterfly, *tie* (tee eh), sounds like the word meaning 70 or 80, an age considered extremely old in ancient times.) Most Tang poets wrote in a form known as Regulated Verse in which each line had either five or seven words.

Fortunately, a huge number of poems written during this highly creative period have survived to our own times. A collection of Tang poetry published in 1707 contains 50,000 poems. (Poetry continues to be popular in China. About 3,000 of the Tang poems are familiar to the typical educated Chinese person today.)

Two of the greatest Tang poets were Li Bo and Du Fu. Both were members of the Hanlin Academy. Although they were good friends, their temperaments and attitudes couldn't have been more different.

Li Bo (701-762) was a Daoist, a pleasure lover, and a favorite of the royal court. He was a tall and agile man, who handled a sword with skill and enjoyed being surrounded by his friends. He formed a group known as the "Eight Immortals of the Wine Cup." They would gather together in the evening, sip wine, and share the poems they had written. (They had much in common with the Seven Sages of the Bamboo Grove!) Many of Li Bo's poems describe the delights of these moonlight parties, the taste of good wine, and the joys of listening to music. In one, he writes, "Forever committed to carefree play, we'll all meet again in the Milky Way!" Others reflect his sadness as he muses about being far from home.

Sometimes the poet got into fights after imbibing too much wine. According to legend, he became tipsy one night and leaned out the boat he was in to give the moon a hug. He fell into the water and drowned. Happily, he left behind 20,000 poems, of which 1,800 have survived to the present.

Du Fu ((712-770) was a serious, even solemn, man, a devout follower of the teachings of Confucius. He had personally experienced the darker side of life, having failed in the civil examinations, and this left him with a long-lasting feeling of disappointment (as well as a need to struggle to make a living).

Du Fu's carefully written lyrics reflect

By Tang times, ink (soot mixed with glue) came in dried little blocks. To use it a writer rubbed the block on an inkstone (a flat rock with a little bowl in one end). He added water to the bowl and stirred the ink powder and the water with his brush. There were three main styles of writing: regular, running and grass. Regular style was standard, block-like letters. Running style was similar to cursive, the letters seeming to run across the paper. Grass style was more elegant and artistic-looking. A good calligrapher mastered all three, after many years of hard work and practice.

NIGHT THOUGHTS   by Li Bo

The bright moon shone before my bed,

I wondered — was it frost upon the ground?

I raised my head to gaze at the clear moon,

Bowed my head, remembering my old home.

his deep awareness of the suffering and tragedy of human life, as well as his disgust for the evils of warfare and political corruption. He also wrote a few verses about wine, although, as you would expect, these certainly lack the carefree spirit of Li Po's. About 1,500 of Du Fu's poems have survived.

Landscape Painting

Landscape painting first became popular during the Eastern Han period, when artists, fleeing from the wars in the north, found a haven in the beautiful Yangzi River valley. Xuanzong encouraged the development of this type of painting in his court.

Before we continue, a few words should be said about Chinese painting. Unlike most familiar works in Western art, Chinese paintings are generally two-dimensional. (They depict length and width but not depth, so they lack a sense of perspective.) Close objects appear at the bottom, while those in the distance are painted at the top. There is a sense of unity and harmony between human beings and the world of nature. And while a Western picture fills the entire frame, a Chinese work has blank spaces that seem to complement or balance the figures. Simplicity, elegance, and symbolism are the key words in Chinese art.

Like the poets, the artists of the Tang dynasty were drawn from the ranks of the scholar/officials. They were not professionals; they simply painted to express their innermost feelings. An artist used the same materials as he would for writing — a brush pen, ink (and sometimes water-based paints), and paper or silk. Since the paper (or silk) quickly absorbed the ink or paint, the artist had to plan his figures well, drawing his lines with skill and a steady hand. He had no chance to change something he didn't like. If he "messed up," he had to start all over again. Artists often painted on horizontal scrolls, which were rolled up when not in use. A scroll was a lot like a picture book. It was divided into sections, with scenes of figures alternating with pure landscape. A viewer unrolled the scroll from right to left, letting the right side roll up again as he progressed through the story told by the various scenes all the way to the end, at the very left side. Then he would reroll it from left to right, so that it would be ready to be viewed by someone else. (In this way, a scroll was like a tape for a modern VCR. People who rent tapes are reminded to "be kind and rewind.")

Wang Wei was painter as well as a poet, musician, and scholar — in many ways the ideal (multi-talented) Tang courtier. He is particularly known for his beautiful winter landscapes, with their towering mountains and gently flowing rivers. When people appear in one of his paintings, they seem very small and diminutive amidst the majesty of the natural world. Wang also experimented with monochrome ink paint-

ings, which featured black figures silhouetted against a white background. These elegantly simple pieces were intended to capture a mood, like a poem. And as in poetry, the landscapes were filled with symbolism.

During the Tang dynasty, landscape painting became closely associated with calligraphy (beautiful handwriting). A short poetic description of a painting was written in beautiful characters in the upper right hand corner. In this way, art, poetry, and calligraphy blended together in a single work.

Wu Daozi (woo dao-zuh) devoted his career to painting very realistic murals for temples and monasteries, skillfully capturing the lifelike qualities of the sculpted statues of India with his paintbrush. Wu's bold brush strokes contrasted with the delicate brushwork of the other artists. His images seemed to pulsate with life — the viewer almost expected the horses to gallop out of his paintings or the birds to suddenly take flight! For this reason, he has been referred

Plants were often used as symbols in art and religion. A favorite landscape motif was a grouping of the "three friends of winter." These "friends" were the bamboo, plum blossom, and pine tree.

The bamboo was revered for its ability to bend with the wind, yet remain upright. Its hollow stem created the sense of being "impartial," or free of prejudice. So the bamboo came to symbolize strength and long-lasting friendship. The plum tree was the first to blossom in spring, and for this reason it was associated with renewal and rebirth. The pine tree remains green and stately during the harshest winter storms. It symbolized inner strength and longevity.

A landscape featuring the "three friends of winter" was thus not merely a glimpse of natural beauty — it was also a philosophical statement.

to as the Michelangelo of China. Thousands of people used to gather to watch him paint his murals.

Storytellers described how Wu Daozi left this earth by disappearing into one of his own paintings. Sadly, none of his work survives. However, the artists who painted frescoes on the cave walls at Dunhuang shortly after his death were clearly influenced by his style.

Ceramics

The Tang dynasty is also famous for beautiful ceramic statues. In fact, Tang craftsmen produced the only substantial group of secular (non-religious) statues that exist from dynastic China. Their delicate figures of courtiers, ladies, musicians, and dancers vividly bring to life the court of this fascinating period. Many of these have survived in good condition to the present day because they were carefully placed in the tombs of the wealthy.

Unlike earlier Chinese statues, which were often stiff and unrealistic, the Tang figures are very lifelike and seem to exude tremendous energy. The women fall into two categories — some are slender while others are quite plump. (Historians tell us that the plump figures were popular after Xuanzong became infatuated with Lady Yang, a woman of ample proportions!) Other favorite subjects were horses — depicted as vigorous steeds, ready to spring

into action — and camels, patiently bearing heavy loads of silk and spices. As in Han times, clay models of buildings, such as houses and granaries, were placed in the tombs for the nobleman's spirit to inhabit in the afterlife. Fierce guardian spirits stood near the entrance to a tomb to frighten away looming demons.

Craftsmen molded the figures from white clay (kaolin), covered them with a cream glaze, and fired them in a kiln. Then they covered them with a second glaze, to which pigments were added (copper for green, cobalt for deep blue, and iron oxide for shades from amber to soft yellow). When fired, the colors intermingled and fused, producing an interesting effect. These figures are known as "three-color ware" (*sancai*).

Certain artists specialized in figures of Buddha. Given the tastes of the age (remember those plump women), these Buddhas were rather portly. They had full cheeks, fleshy lips, and the chin and neck grooved to suggest "an opulence of flesh." The folds of the drapery fell naturally over the rotund figure.

The most highly prized Tang ceramics were white porcelains, which were produced mainly in Hebei province. They were very thin and translucent. Some were as transparent as glass — water could be seen through them. These were referred to as "disks of thinnest ice" Archaeologists have found sets of 10 white bowls from Xingzhou that could be struck with little ebony rods and used as chimes.

New techniques were developed by Tang potters for decorating the white glaze by painting or stamping them with brightly colored designs. In later centuries, elaborately decorated porcelain would be one of China's greatest treasures.

A Love of Horses

The many ceramic horses that have been found give us a good idea of how greatly these animals were admired in Tang society. As you know, the feisty, long-legged horses of Ferghana were first brought into China during the Western Han period. When the Tang dynasty began, there were only about 5,000 horses in China, mostly in Gansu province. Taizong's ambitious military campaigns required more horses for his cavalry. Within 50 years, the number had increased to over 700,000, as a result of aggressive breeding programs as well as gifts of tribute. Each horse was assigned to a herd of 120 animals. The herds were kept in pastoral "inspectorates" of 50,000 horses. Every animal was branded with the character meaning "official" as well as those indicating its origin, quality (flying, dragon, or wind), class of work (war, post, or royal

Horseback riding was reserved for the nobility: an edict of 667 prohibited merchants and artisans from riding.

mount) and the name of its inspectorate.

Taizong had his six favorite war steeds commemorated in verse, painted by court painter Yan Liben and carved in stone for his tomb. Gaozong placed a colossal pair of winged horses at the start of the spirit roads leading to his place of burial. Xuanzong kept thousands of horses in the imperial stables. One of the most famous of all Chinese paintings, *Shining White of the Night*, is a depiction of his favorite steed by artist Han Gan.

Courtiers and ladies of the court often rode horseback for pleasure and hunting. Polo was a favorite game played by teams of riders who competed to drive a ball with mallets into a goal. Polo originated in Persia 4,000 years ago and was brought to China via the Silk Road around the 5th century. Xuanzong enjoyed polo so much that he often neglected his imperial duties. Matches were held on the palace grounds at Chang'an. There was great rejoicing when the emperor's team of four players beat a team of ten from Tibet.

Some horses were trained to dance at court! They were arrayed in blankets of embroidered silk fringed with gold and silver threads, their manes studded with precious stones. They often had horns attached

to their heads (to represent unicorns) and wings tied to their backs. The horses "danced" intricate maneuvers, often circling around while keeping their hind legs in one spot, or advancing together in rhythmic steps to the center of a large banquet room, where they picked up golden bowls filled with wine in their teeth. (In 1970 a magnificent silver flask was found in a Tang tomb decorated with a picture of a dancing horse holding just such a bowl.) Xuanzong was entertained on his birthday one year by 100 of the finest dancing horses, their heads tossing and tails swishing to the beat of the music.

The horse is one of the 12 animals in the Chinese zodiac. People born in the Year of the Horse are thought to be cheerful, independent, clever, talkative, quick to anger, and able to handle money well. A bright young Chinese scholar is traditionally called a "thousand *li* colt."

The Everlasting Regret

At the end of a most illustrious career, an aging Xuanzong became obsessed with a beautiful concubine, Yang Guifei (yong kway fay). (This is the woman who inspired all those plump ceramic figures!) He pampered her in every way — even to the point of having her favorite snack, litchi nuts, delivered to her daily. (Litchi nuts had to be imported from a thousand miles away!) From the beginning, Yang Guifei took advantage of her powers over the emperor to place her friends and relatives in high government positions. She helped her cousin, Yang Guozhong, become chief minister of the Secretariat, even though many people found him lacking in political skill.

In 751 Yang Guifei was charmed by An Lushan, a professional soldier from the northeast who rose in the ranks to general. Ten years earlier he had become the military governor of a sector along the frontier. His successful campaigns won him great praise from the emperor. Despite his rather ugly appearance — he was grossly fat! — he became a favorite of the court. (Part of his appeal lay in his wit and vivid sense of humor.) Yang Guifei was so taken with him that she adopted him as her son! This aroused the jealousy of Yang Guozhong (her cousin, the chief minister), who saw him as a threat to his own position. The minister was further enraged when Xuanzong appointed An Lushan governor of Hubei province, (this, of course, was largely Yang Guifei's doing), and he tried to turn the emperor against the portly general.

The conflict between the two men raged until, in 755, An Lushan marched south with an army of 150,000 men and seized Luoyang. And he didn't stop there. He declared himself founder of a new dynasty. (Known as the Great Yan, his dynasty would never be included among the dynasties recognized by the official historians).

Xuanzong knew he was in trouble when An Lushan started moving toward Chang'an. As his enemy approached, he fled under the cover of night, accompanied by Yang Guifei and Yang Guozhong. They headed for Chengdu in Sichuan. When their route was blocked by Tibetan troops, their escort suddenly mutinied. The soldiers blamed the empire's troubles on the beautiful Yang Guifei and her inept cousin. They murdered Yang Guozhong on the spot and then shifted their focus to Yang Guifei.

The weeping emperor was forced to order the execution of his beloved concubine. She was strangled with a silk cord in a nearby village pagoda. Xuanzong then continued his journey, alone. Later that year, he abdicated in favor of his son, who had fled from Chang'an to the northwest to raise military support.

The poignant scene of Xuanzong's flight from Chang'an was immortalized in a romantic epic poem, *Song of Everlasting Regret*. Written by Bo Yuyi in the 9th century, it became one of the most beloved poems in all of Chinese literature. Yang Guifei has been known ever after as a siren — an evil woman who destroys the men who are drawn to her. (She joined the ranks of the Empresses Lu and Wu!)

Artist Li Sixun painted *Ming Haung's Journey to Shu*, a haunting landscape in blues and greens that depicts the flight of the emperor. Later dynasties would write other poems as well as plays, and even operas, about Yang Guifei. In 1993, a 40-part series about her entitled *Concubine Yang* was produced on Chinese television.

Death of an Emperor

By the time Suzong (Xuanzong's son) took the throne, Chang'an and Luoyang were under Tang rule again. A year later, Xuanzong returned to the capital, where he lived a simple life as the "retired emperor." The "Brilliant Emperor" died in his palace in 761 at the age of 77, a shadow of his former self.

Although the Tang dynasty would continue for two more centuries, it never recovered from An Lushan's rebellion. The height of its power was over, and the emperors who reigned during the rest of the dynasty lacked the talent and political authority of the rulers who had preceded them.

The Arts in the Later Years

Despite the dwindling of imperial majesty, the arts continued to thrive. (Have you noticed how Chinese culture managed to flourish and evolve in even the most chaotic of times?) Most of the Tang rulers were patrons of poetry and music. Several even had considerable creative ability.

Drama made some important inroads about this time. For centuries, troops of men and women had made a living by acting out stories and folk tales in the marketplaces in Chang'an and other cities. By the later years of the Tang dynasty, acting troops were presenting well-structured song-and-dance "plays," which were highlighted by acrobatics. They dressed in elaborate costumes and performed on raised platforms. The audience had to watch the actors closely, since there was no scenery, nor were there stage props.

The Printed Page

As you know, Chinese writing and record-keeping dates from very ancient times. But imagine how tedious it must have been to copy long materials by hand, character by character. Many scribes must have wondered how it could be made easier. As was often true in China, the answer lay in the past.

During the Han Dynasty, the great Confucian classics had been carved on a series of stones. (This project involved carving over two hundred thousand characters.) Scholars and artisans often made ink rubbings of these writings by carefully fitting damp paper over the stone inscription and patting the surface with soot. The soot adhered to everything except the indented characters. The result was a white-on-black picture of the original.

In later years officials began using seals made from bronze, stone, or wood, upon which an inscription was carved — in reverse. They were pressed into red ink paste and stamped on official documents. These "stamps" often replaced signatures on letters and documents. (They still do today!)

During the Tang dynasty, this technique was applied to book-making. Here's how it was done. The text was painted with thick black strokes on very fine paper and pasted, front side down, onto a wooden block. (The writing could easily be seen through the paper.) Then the background was cut away on the wood, leaving the raised characters, which, of course, appeared in reverse. Illustrations could also be carved into the wood. The printer inked the surface of the block and pressed paper sheets against it to produce a copy of the text. He could produce 1,500 copies a day. Each wooden block yielded 20,000 copies before it had to be replaced.

By 700 AD block printing was well on its way to becoming a major industry in China. Carved wooden blocks were used to make calendars, scholarly books, government documents, poetry collections, and novels. The demand for copies of the classics to study for civil service exams further stimulated the growth of print-making.

The world's oldest surviving complete woodblock book was printed in China on May 11, 868. It is a copy of a Buddhist scripture called the Diamond Sutra. It does not look at all like a modern book. Rather, it is a 17-foot long scroll made from six sheets of paper pasted together. It includes both text and pictures.

The first bound books were made in the later years of the Tang dynasty. Their pages were glued to a spine. Gradually, these books would replace the scrolls.

Around 900 the government began issuing "flying money" - paper certificates for government purchases. This was the world's first paper money. It was issued in order to reduce transport costs — one mule load of paper equaled 40 mule loads of coins.

Attacks Upon Buddhism

Buddhism reached its high point in China around 700. By then, several distinct sects had emerged, and thousands of monasteries had been built throughout the country on tax-free land given by wealthy believers. Many of these monasteries became centers of learning, and everyone flocked to them for the many festivals held there.

During the early years of the Tang, Buddhism, Confucianism and Daoism coexisted as the "Three Teachings" of Chinese culture. Confucianism was closely connected with family rituals, and Daoism was associated with practices for good health. (Think about all those breathing and movement exercises, acupuncture, and even *feng shui*.) And despite Gaozu's lack of support at the beginning of the dynasty, Buddhism continued to grow, encouraging people to be compassionate and seek inner peace. Every day, the yellow-clad monks in the monasteries sang services for the dead before a large statue of Buddha.

But during the later years of the dynasty, certain people began complaining that Buddhism conflicted with the principles of Confucianism. Han Yu was a high-ranking official, who was also a poet, scholar, and the greatest prose writer of his time. Han was an ardent Confucianist, and he distrusted many Buddhist beliefs. He par-

ticularly opposed the belief in relics (body parts that supposedly belonged to the Buddha himself). When a finger bone attributed to Buddha was put on display in the imperial palace in Chang'an, Han wrote an essay (*On the Bone of Buddha*) protesting what he called "the superstitious nature of a foreign religion." He later wrote that the government should outlaw Buddhism, which he blamed for "stirring up trouble" ever since its arrival in China. To hush him up and avoid conflict, he was promptly sent into exile.

But other people were also concerned about the influence of Buddhism on Chinese culture. Many worried about the growing wealth and independence of the monasteries. Although the monks contributed to the well-being of the community by running hospitals and providing food grown in their gardens for the sick and poor, many of the monasteries seemed like little self-sufficient kingdoms. Some of the government officials looked for ways to tax them, and it was rumored that many of the monasteries' precious art objects were seized for the emperor's treasury.

In the 840's a mentally unstable emperor, Wuzong, began a full-scale attack upon the Buddhists. He was obsessed with his quest for immortality, and many historians believe his mind was harmed by the potions he was constantly drinking. Either because of temporary madness, or, more likely, because he needed to replenish his treasury, he ordered the destruction of 40,000 shrines and 4,600 monasteries. He also forced 260,000 monks and nuns to give up their religious practices and return to ordinary life.

The artistic loss was immeasurable. (This is when the wonderful paintings of Wu Daozi were destroyed.) Bronze statuary was melted down for coinage, iron was reclaimed for agricultural tools, while gold, silver, and other precious metals were placed in the imperial treasury.

Wuzong's successor brought an end to the attack upon Buddhism. But although the religion survived, it played a lesser role in Chinese culture than it had in the past.

Fireworks Enliven the Show

Gunpowder is a Chinese invention that has had an immeasurable effect upon world history. The formula was discovered — by accident — around 800, when some Daoist alchemists, seeking a way of converting base metals into gold, mixed together charcoal, sulfur and saltpeter. When they ignited this substance, it exploded!

For a long time, gunpowder was used for festivals. It was stuffed into hollow sticks of bamboo, ignited, and thrown up into the air to make a loud noise. Later, color was added to the formula. Indigo was used to make blue-green, white lead carbonate to make white, red lead tetroxide to make red, cinnabar to make purple, and arsenic sulphides to make yellow. Powdered cast-iron shavings added bright sparkles. These "fireworks" were launched into the sky to make colorful designs along with loud noises.

Firecrackers and fireworks were closely associated with the most important holiday in China — the New Year — which begins on the first full moon after January 21. An ancient Chinese legend explains the use of explosives during the New Year's festivities. It seems that a long time ago there

---

The New Year's festival is still China's most important holiday. It lasts 15 days. On the third day a parade of dancers carrying a lone dragon weave through the streets. The dragon has a large wooden head and a long, colorful body made of silk. It is so huge that it takes two people to hold up the head and twelve more to act as his legs (dancing beneath the cloth body). They are accompanied by crashing cymbals and loud, crackling bamboo firecrackers to scare away the evil spirits. As the dragon passes the houses, people open their doors to let in the good luck it brings. Friends and family members shout to one another, "Gongxi Facai (Goong-shee Fah-tsai), which is Mandarin for "I wish you happiness and prosperity."

(The Dragon Dance originated as a ritual designed to encourage rain.)

had been a monster who ate people. The gods decided to lock him up inside a mountain to protect the people from being devoured. Once a year, however, during the New Year's festival, the gods allowed him to come out. So the Chinese lit firecrackers to frighten him and keep him away from their houses.

The Fall of the Tang

After 820, the government of China became very weak. A series of young emperors were so ineffective that no one even listened to them. (This was usually a sign of the end of a dynasty.) Many factions fought for power, among them groups of eunuchs. The last three emperors were little more than puppets manipulated by the chief eunuch, Tian Lingzi.

In 874, a rebellion broke out among angry peasants in the region between the Yellow and Huai rivers. Already overburdened by heavy taxes, the people had suffered through a succession of floods and droughts. They wanted a new government that would help them, not tax them. The revolt was spurred on by gangs of bandits. One of these, led by Huang Chao, swept south and sacked the city of Guangzhou. He slaughtered 120,00 of the 200,000 foreign merchants. When he headed for Chang'an, the emperor fled for his life to Chengdu. (Sound familiar?) In 880 he captured the Tang capital.

Huang Chao founded a new dynasty, but he had no idea how to form a government. His talents lay in destruction, not construction! In fact, his manner was so brutal that his own forces turned against him and killed him in 884. So much for that dynasty.

Although the Tang emperor returned to Chang'an, his influence, such as it was, remained limited to the region surrounding the city. His dynasty was breathing its last gasps. Lacking a strong central government, the governors in the provinces started making their own decisions. Many districts in central and south China actually seceded and formed independent states.

Finally, in 904 a military commander (Zhu Wen) killed the Tang emperor and placed his heir on the throne. Three years later, the same man usurped the throne, proclaiming himself emperor of a new dynasty, the Liang. (Another one!) The Tang dynasty had come to an end.

Afterwards

China remained in a state of turmoil for about 50 years, until unity was finally restored with the founding of the Song dynasty. This dynasty would last a long time and reestablish the political institutions created by the Han and strengthened by the Tang. Here was proof of the strength and endurance of the Chinese form of government.

Review Questions

1. Had did Gaozu deal with the surviving members of the Sui dynasty?
2. Why did Taizong claim that he was the Grand Ancestor of the Tang?
3. Describe the expanding empire under Taizong.
4. What was the basic plan of Chang'an?
5. What did the colors white, red, and yellow symbolize?
6. What was Xuan Zang's greatest legacy to China?
7. How would you rate Empress Wu as a ruler? Explain your answer.
8. Why is Xuanzong called "the Brilliant Emperor?"
9. Compare Li Bo to Du Fu.
10. What was so special about Wu Daozi?
11. What was "three color ware?"
12. How did horses entertain the Tang court?
13. What was the story connected with "the everlasting regret?"
14. What are *fan* and *cai*?
15. What was the first printed book in China?
16. Why do you think Wuzong attacked the Buddhist monasteries?
17. How was gunpowder invented?
18. What was the main use of gunpowder in Tang China?
19. What were some of the causes of the fall of the Tang dynasty?

Projects

1. Find out about Queen Hatshepsut of ancient Egypt. Then write a paper comparing her to Empress Wu Zetian.

2. Fierce-looking terracotta figures guarded the Tang tombs from monstrous demons. These creatures, often shown in pairs, were associated with the *lokapala*, the protectors of the Buddhas found in cave temples. They sometimes appeared as hybrid creatures with a human or animal face, fierce expression, a strong winged torso and hooves. Look in some books on Chinese art for examples of these tomb guardians. Draw one or make a clay model.

3. Phoenix was the Greek name for the mythological bird (Bennu) that was sacred to the ancient Egyptian sun god. It represented the sun, which died in its own flames each evening and emerged, reborn, each morning. From this tradition grew a myth about a bird that lived in Arabia that had a life span of 500 years, after which it built a nest, set it afire, and perished in the flames. From the ashes arose a new phoenix. Do some research and find out if this Greek myth had anything to do with the Chinese phoenix. Then write a report about the role of the phoenix in eastern and western cultures.

4. Try printing with a raw potato. Cut a potato in half and carve a design into the white flesh of the vegetable. Then dip it in a pie plate filled with paint and print the design on a piece of paper. Try making your initials this way — remember, they must be cut in reverse on your potato block.

5. A huge dam is currently under construction where the Yangzi River winds through the cliffs of the Three Gorges area in southern China. It will be the world's largest hydroelectric dam, redirecting the river and creating a lake 375 feet deep. The dam will help control the river's floodwaters while providing electricity. However, its construction will flood 13 cities, 140 towns and 300 villages – forcing over a million people to move.

The waters will cover as many as 500 unstudied archaeological sites that contain important information about China's past. This includes more than 300,000 characters were carved into the White Crane Ridge above the Yangzi beginning in the Tang dynasty and until as recently as the 20th century. Three massive stone pillars that are important Han relics will also be lost.

Archaeologists around the world are racing against time to preserve as many sites as possible, but many already lost to the rising waters of the dam. (A similar situation occurred in Egypt when the Aswan dam was built.) This project will be finished in another decade.

Find out more about this project. Then set up a debate with several classmates. One team should argue in favor of building the dam (explain the benefits for society), while the other team should give reasons why the dam should not be built. After listening to the debate, the rest of the class should vote on which side presented the strongest argument.

6. The Lantern Festival originated during the Tang dynasty. Find out what it is and write a short report or make a poster.

7. In the 8th century Buddhist astronomer-monk Yixing used measurements of shadow lengths to calculate the circumference of the earth with surprising accuracy. (Greek Erotosthenes several centuries earlier used the same method.) Find out more about this scientist and write a report.

8. Using popsicle sticks, clay, and cardboard (or other available materials), make a model of Chang'an as it looked during the early Tang dynasty.

9. Find a book of Chinese poetry and read some verses by Li Bo and Du Fu. Select three from each poet to read to your class.

10. Write a skit about "the Everlasting Regret." It can be corny!

11. Find a book containing European landscape paintings from the 19th century. The works of John Constable are perfect for this activity. Then find landscape paintings from the Tang period. Or better still, go to a museum that has these types of paintings. Think about whether a painting depicts a specific place or seems more like the artist's vision, how much of the surface is covered, whether there is perspective, the absence of presence of shadows and/or of writing. Make a list of comparisons and contrasts.

12. Have a class banquet, Chinese style!

13. Write a report entitled "Famous Women of Ancient Chinese History."

14. Use a sheet of absorbent paper and a brush pen (pen-like markers) to make a Chinese style landscape painting. No first sketch. Think first, then paint. Write a poem about the picture in one corner.

15. Adopt a Tang identity: become an official, artist, or farmer. Write about a day in your life.

16. Robert Van Gulik wrote several detective stories set during the Tang dynasty. See if you can find some. (He died in 1967, but they are still in print.)

17. Search in the art books in the library or on the Internet for the painting, "Shining White of the Night" by Han Gan. Study the painting. Then write a poem to go with it.

19. You've learned quite a bit about Chang'an in this book. Find out more about the history of this ancient city (it's modern name is Xian), and write a report. Be sure to include a timeline and illustrations.

20. As a review of everything you've learned in this book, make a timeline indicating the major accomplishments and events of Chinese history, beginning with the Shang dynasty.

Happenings Elsewhere in the World During the Tang Dynasty

Kingdom of Ghana established (c 600)

Rise of Arab empire (635 – 715)

Charlemagne (768 – 814)

Beginnings of feudalism in Europe

Golden age of the Mayan civilization

EPILOGUE
THE LEGACY OF ANCIENT CHINA

Here we are at the end of the story of ancient China. Isn't it amazing how much happened in that distant part of the world long, long ago? It's a fascinating story, but you might be feeling a bit dazzled by the huge amount of information contained in this book. To help you grasp the "big picture," let's review some of the major themes running through it.

Let's begin with the strong sense of national pride. As you know, the Chinese considered their Middle Kingdom the center of the earth. Even when contact was made with such distant places as Korea, India, and even Rome, they continued to believe that theirs was the most highly civilized country in the world.

Closely tied to this sense of national pride was a long tradition of recording important events. As early as the Shang dynasty, scribes were keeping records of the king's activities. *The Book of Documents* and the volumes of Sima Qian are early indicators of how highly the Chinese valued historical records. What is also intriguing is the way the Chinese viewed their history in terms of cycles — a dynasty would be founded, evolve, and flourish, until one of the rulers lost his mandate to govern. At this point, the people would revolt and chaos would reign until someone else came along to start a new dynasty. This is very different from the western approach, which views history as progressing steadily upwards along a slanting line.

The need for records promoted the development of a system of writing. And the richness of the written language enabled poets to create some wonderful, deeply personal verses. Once paper was invented, the written word was more widely distributed, and the development of the printing process further increased the spread of knowledge throughout China.

The tradition of record-keeping and the value placed upon intellect helped produce a very talented class of government official. Beginning in Han times, academies were founded in the major cities, and the Civil Service Examinations provided the government with a good supply of men well-educated in the great classics. These men ran an extremely efficient bureaucracy, which had been designed by Shi Huangdi and was refined by the Han and the Tang. It survived many periods of political unrest and endured until fairly recent times.

One reason why the government functioned so well was the tradition of respect for authority and the long-standing preference for a social hierarchy. The ranks of status were based upon those of the family, and Chinese society was viewed as an extended family headed by the emperor. The rules set out by Confucius helped maintain order and stability in China for over two thousand years.

Confucianism, of course, was one of the "big three" ideologies in ancient China. While it stressed social harmony, Daoism encouraged its followers to be attuned to the flow of nature. Buddhism, on the other hand, stressed compassion, meditation, and performing good deeds. Even today, the strengths of each of these ideologies continue to influence and enrich Chinese culture.

History, writing, education, and philosophy are important threads running through the story of ancient China. So is art. You've seen how since very early times Chinese craftsmen created a variety of beautiful objects, working with clay, bronze, jade, lacquer, and stone. Beautiful brush paintings date from the early Han period (remember the shroud covering the coffin of the Countess of Dai?). The landscapes of the Tang period are among the great masterpieces of the world.

And just think about Chinese ingenuity. Clever people living in those ancient times invented the compass, the wheelbarrow, the kite, the umbrella, the seismoscope, gunpowder, and much, much more.

These are some of the main threads running through ancient Chinese civilization. Perhaps you can think of others. And this is only part of the "big picture." We haven't even mentioned the colorful characters who made everything happen — the emperors, generals, artists, concubines, eunuchs, bandits, ministers... and the list goes on.

One thing is certain. The people of ancient China created one of the richest civilizations in the world, and their descendants have much to be proud of. By learning about their history and culture, you will be better prepared to understand and appreciate China's role in the modern world.

TIMELINE

TIMELINE

Neolithic Period	c.7000 — 1750 BC
Xia	c. 2200 — 1750 BC
Shang Dynasty	1750 — 1027 BC
Western Zhou Dynasty	1022 — 771 BC
Eastern Zhou Dynasty	770 — 256 BC

Spring and Autumn Period	770 — 476 BC
Warring States Period	475 — 221 BC

Qin Dynasty	221 — 206 BC
Western Han Dynasty	202 BC — 8 AD
Xin Dynasty	9 — 24
Eastern Han Dynasty	25 — 220
The Age of Division	220 — 581

Three Kingdoms	220 — 265
Western Jin Empire	280 — 304
Period of Disunion	304 — 581

Sui Dynasty	581 — 618
Tang Dynasty	618 — 907

GLOSSARY

Acupuncture - ancient practice of treating disease by inserting needles at precise pints in the body

Alchemist – a person who seeks to change base metals into gold and searches for the elixir of life

Ba Gua - mystical eight trigrams, the key to knowledge, invented by Fuxi

Bodhisattva – follower of Buddha who has achieved enlightment but chosen to remain in the world to help others on the path to sanctity instead of reaching eternal bliss in Nirvana

Bureaucracy - a government divided into departments and divisions and managed by appointed (or elected) officials

Calligraphy - the art of beautiful handwriting

Celadon – ceramics fired at high temperature, coated in a translucent glaze in various shades of green based on iron oxides

Concubine - a woman who lives with an emperor, king, or noble, and has his children but does not have the rights or position of wife

Dao – "the Way" – to Daoists, the primary source of the universe and of life, which permeates and transforms every living being, constantly in motion

Dynasty - a series of rulers who are members of the same family

Eunuch - a castrated man who cares for the wives and concubines of a ruler

Feng Huang – the phoenix, a mythical bird which represented the element fire, the cardinal direction of south, and the season summer; was identified with yin and the empress

Feng Shui - arrangements of objects in accordance with the universe so as to harness the qi in the natural world.

Filial piety — obligations owed to ones parents and ancestors according to rules of Confucius

Glaze – thin, glassy coating, usually shiny and translucent, which covers the surface of certain ceramics

Hierarchy - a group of persons or things arranged in order of rank

Huangdi – Huang and Di were honorary titles given mythical rulers and founders of civilization. The First Emperor conferred upon himself the title Shi (first) Huangdi to emphasize the birth of a new era which was supposed to last forever

Karma — Indian (Hindu and Buddhist) belief in a force generated by a person's good and bad actions that will determine his place in the next life

Mingqi – tomb objects of great symbolic value, mainly made of terracota or wood but occasionally also of metal, placed in tomb to recreate a familiar atmosphere for the deceased and to satisfy his or her needs in the afterlife

Mudra – position of the hands of Buddha or Bodhisattva – the hand open, facing upwards, with palm forward in sign of protection and other hand turned downwards in sign of charity or blessing

Nirvana – for India Buddhists a blessed state where one's soul is oblivious to care and pain, for Chinese Buddhists a kind of heavenly paradise achieved after a life a good works

Porcelain – finest quality of pottery with hard and shiny surface, made of kaolin baked at an extremely high temperature

Qi— life force existing in animate and inanimate objects, needs to be harnessed correctly to avoid imbalance and disharmony

Qilin – unicorn-like animal hybrid and living embodiment of the union of yin and yang – an appearance of such a beast was usually a good omen

Rang – part of Daoist belief, meaning desire to yield, to "go with the flow"

Ren — Virtue, or a concern for other people

Silk Road – overland trading route that stretched from northern China through Asia to Europe

Tian – "Heaven," the greatest divinity from the Zhou period onwards

Wang – Noble title, roughly translated as "king"

Yang – one of two forces of the universe (the other is yin) - associated with everything male, bright, positive, active, etc.

Yin – one of two forces of the universe (the other is yang) - associated with everything female, dark, passive, negative, etc.

THE CHINESE ZODIAC

Western astrologers predict a person's fortune by observing the location of the stars and planets on the day of his/her birth. The ancient Chinese, on the other hand, predicted that people born in a certain year would have a certain set of characteristics. As you learned in Chapter 1, there was a cycle of twelve years in the Chinese calendar, each named after a particular animal. The people born in the year of a certain animal were believed to have some of the characteristics of that animal. Look at the chart below to see what traits you, your friends, and your family members have. Are there any characteristics that should be added to describe your personality?

Year	Characteristics
Year of the Rat 1948, 1960, 1972, 1984, 1996, 2008	You are imaginative, charmy, and truly generous to your friends. However, you can be quick-tempered and critical. You take advantage of opportunities. Good professions for a rat: writer, critic, publicist, musician. Famous rats: Shakespeare, Mozart, Churchill, George Washington, and Truman Capote
Year of the Ox 1949, 1961, 1973, 1985, 1997, 2009	You are dependable and calm, until angered. You inspire confidence and are a good leader. However, you can be stubborn. Good professions for an ox: surgeon, general, hairdresser. Famous oxen: Napoleon, Van Gogh, Walt Disney, Richard Nixon
Year of the Tiger 1950, 1962, 1974, 1986, 1998, 2010	You are sensitive, emotional, and courageous. You have a great sense of adventure. However, you can be self-absorbed and suspicious of others. Good professions for a tiger: explorer, race car driver, CEO. Famous tigers: Marco Polo, Mary, Queen of Scots, Dwight Eisenhower, Marilyn Monroe.
Year of the Rabbit 1951, 1963, 1975, 1987, 1999, 2011	You are friendly, affectionate, and well-liked. People feel they can confide in you. However, you can be too sentimental and appear superficial. Good professions for a rabbit: diplomat, social worker, actor. Famous rabbits: Rudolph Nureyev, Confucius, Orson Welles, Einstein
Year of the Dragon 1952, 1964, 1976, 1988, 2000, 2012	You are healthy, energetic, and enthusiastic. You are intelligent, gifted, and a perfectionist. You can be foolhardy and overly demanding. Good professions for a dragon: artist, politican, scholar. Famous dragons: Joan of Arc, Pearl Buck, Freud

Year	Characteristics
Year of the Snake 1941, 1953, 1965, 1977, 1989, 2001	You are quiet, wise, and romantic. You like good books, good food, music, and drama. You have a good sense of humor, but you can be stingy with money. Good professions for a snake: teacher, philosopher, writer, psychiatrist. Famous snakes: Abraham Lincoln, Edgar Allen Poe, Charles Darwin
Year of the Horse 1942, 1954, 1966, 1978, 1990, 2002	You are independent and hard-working. You are cheerful, intelligent, and logical, but you can be selfish. Good professions for a horse: scientist, composer, software designer. Famous horses: Rembrandt, Chopin, Davy Crockett, Teddy Roosevelt
Year of the Sheep 1943, 1955, 1967, 1979, 1991, 2003	You appreciate beauty and elegance. You are very artistic and inquisitive. However, you tend to complain and worry too much. Good professions for a sheep: actor, artist, landscape designer. Famous sheep: Michelangelo, Rudolph Valentino, Mark Twain
Year of the Monkey 1944, 1956, 1968, 1980, 1992, 2004	You are clever and amusing, and you are good at solving problems. You have a magnetic personality. However, you can be impatient or lazy. Good professions for a monkey: TV show host, actor, graphic designer. Famous monkeys: Julius Caesar, Leonardo da Vinci, Harry Truman, Elizabeth Taylor
Year of the Rooster 1945, 1957, 1969, 1981, 1993, 2005	You work hard, think deeply, and make good decisions. You have many talents and are a smart dresser. However, you can be a dreamer or be boastful. Good professions for a rooser: restaurant owner, publicist, general, world traveler. Famous roosters: Groucho Marx, Rudyard Kipling, Caruso (opera singer)
Year of the Dog 1946, 1958, 1970, 1982, 1994, 2006	You have a deep sense of loyalty and duty. You will always keep a secret. However, you sometimes worry too much or are overly critical. Good professions for a dog: teacher, activist, secret agent. Famous dogs: Socrates, Benjamin Franklin, Herbert Hoover
Year of the Boar 1947, 1959, 1971, 1983, 1995, 2007	You are brave, intellectual, and ambitious. You have a strong need to set difficult goals and then achieve them. You are sincere, tolerant, and honest, but you can be very naive. Good professions a boar: entertainer, researcher, explorer. Famous boars: Albert Schweitzer, Ernest Hemingway.

INDEX